Education, Repression & Liberation: Namibia

Education, Repression & Liberation: Namibia

Justin Ellis

World University Service

The Catholic Institute for International Relations

First published in January 1984 by
Catholic Institute for International Relations, 22 Coleman Fields, London
N1 7AF, and
World University Service, 20/21 Compton Terrace, London N1 2UN

©CIIR and World University Service 1984
ISBN 0 904393 78 X CIIR
ISBN 0 906405 10 6 WUS

Ellis, Justin
   Education, repression and liberation: Namibia
   (A Future for Namibia; 4)
   1. Educational sociology — Namibia
   2. Education and state — Namibia
   I. Title   II. Series
   370.19'09688   LC191.8.N/

Edited by: Neil MacDonald and CIIR

Design: Michael Green (01-997-6376) and Skater

Typesetting and printing: Russell Press Ltd, Bertrand Russell House, Nottingham, UK

Trade distribution by Third World Publications Ltd, 151 Stratford Rd, Birmingham B11 1RD, Tel: 021-773-6572

Contents

Preface	7
INTRODUCTION	8
1. EDUCATION THROUGH OPPRESSION	12
2. EDUCATION TODAY	34
3. EDUCATION THROUGH EXILE	54
4. COME INDEPENDENCE	62
Appendix	76
Statistical Supplement	80
Bibliography	88

List of Tables

1. Numbers in Different Classes 1981	80
2. Numbers in School 1971-1981	81
3. Enrolments in Namibia and Botswana 1981	81
4. Analysis of Black Enrolments 1980	82
5. Teacher/Pupil Ratios	83
6. Education Expenditure 1981/82	83
7. Black Teachers' Salaries 1982	84
8. Black Teachers' Qualifications 1980	84
9. Academy for Tertiary Education Enrolments 1981	85
10. Namibian students at South African Universities 1971-78	85
11. Requirements for Skilled Personnel at Independence	86

List of Figures

1. Number of Students in Black Schools 1892-1981	24
2. Proportion of Pupils in Different Classes 1981	35
3. Number of Pupils by Standard and Age 1981	37
4. 1981 Education Expenditure per Pupil	41

List of Illustrations

1. Map of Namibia 9
2. Map of Land Distribution in Namibia 11
3. South African Schooltexts for Namibia: Warlike Blacks and Peaceful Whites 16
4. South African Schooltexts for Namibia: Civilization 22
5. South African Schooltexts for Namibia: White Initiative and Black Labour 32
6. South African Schooltexts for Namibia: Civilization Under Siege 42
7. South African Schooltexts for Namibia: Race 46
8. Material from SWAPO Literacy Campaign: Housing 56
9. Material from SWAPO Literacy Campaign: Decision Making 71

Preface

I am very grateful to the many people who provided information comments or suggestions and read the various drafts of this booklet. In particular, I must pay tribute to WUS and CIIR for the quality of support they have provided. I am indebted to Henning Melber for his thorough study of Namibian education (*Schule und Kolonialismus: das formale Erziehungswesen Namibias*) which has been drawn on for parts of the first two chapters. Prof. R.H. Green of IDS, Sussex University, provided many detailed and useful comments. Regrettably, I am unable to name several others, but I do hope they are pleased with the result.

Justin Ellis

Introduction

As South Africa's colony, Namibia still experiences extremes of exploitation and racism. In Namibian education three separate sectors cater for blacks, whites and 'coloureds'[1]. And within each sector there has been further segregation between ethnic groups in a 'divide and rule' strategy. Expenditure on each white schoolchild has been six to ten times that on each black pupil. The paucity of black education is such that illiteracy among blacks is at least 60% (and blacks are 80% of the population). Black secondary education was so neglected by the South African government that between 1970 and 1979 no more than 300 blacks gained a University Entrance qualification. They were expected to study at black universities in South Africa: Namibia has no university of its own. There has been a similar lack of technical, vocational and teacher training.

Not surprisingly, Namibian schools have been places of conflict. Blacks — particularly in secondary schools — have rebelled against a syllabus they find offensive, and against the oppressive regime of school, and the wider society. Now some schools are partly staffed by young South African soldiers who bring their weapons to the classroom.

This system of education deprives Namibians of the skills they need to govern themselves and develop as a nation. This will continue

---

1. In describing the structures created in Namibia by the South African government it is necessary to use terms such as 'white', 'coloured' (for people of mixed race), and 'black'. The use of the terms here certainly does not imply any acceptance of these South African-imposed divisions. The people thus labelled are not one group just because one name has been imposed on them: each in fact contains several groups and communities, classifed together but often adminstratively separate. 'Coloured' education in particular is an umbrella for three unequal educational structures for Rehobothers, Coloureds and Namas, with Namas receiving a similar standard of education to their fellow black Namibians.

Map 1 Namibia

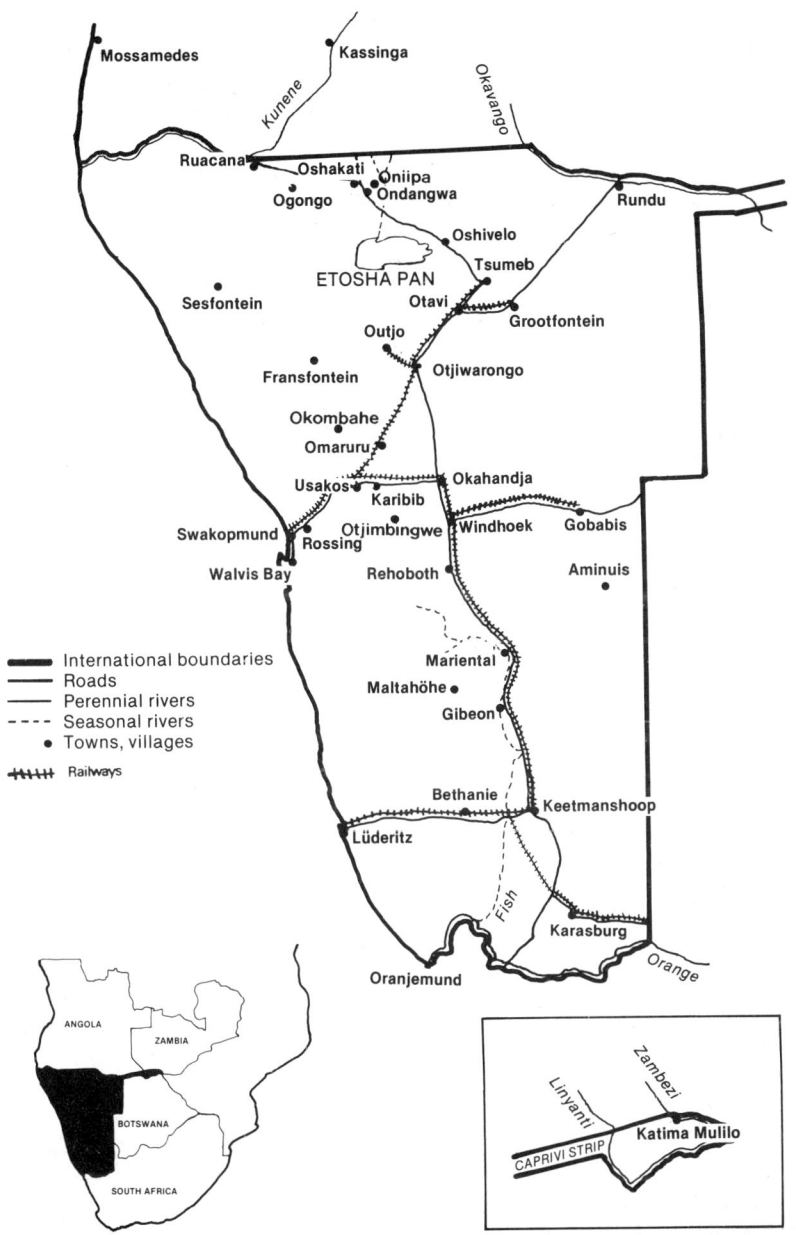

to be the case however long South Africa delays independence. The South West Africa Peoples Organisation (SWAPO) has made progress since 1974 in providing an education for tens of thousands of refugees, and has sent abroad some 5 000 for study at various levels. Many programmes have been set up in exile in preparation for independence, but they cannot make up the enormous backlog of skills.

Namibia is therefore likely to reach independence facing an educational crisis. However, there is reason for optimism: Namibians have started to educate themselves, and can draw on the experiences of other countries which have achieved independence in the past two decades. Opportunities exist for innovation, particularly in adult education, and for relating formal education more closely to developmental needs. Nevertheless, Namibians face some crucial and difficult educational problems, before as well as after independence.

This booklet attempts first to understand the history and function of the education system, and then in the second part to examine future prospects and problems.

Map 2 Land Distribution: Population and Bantustans

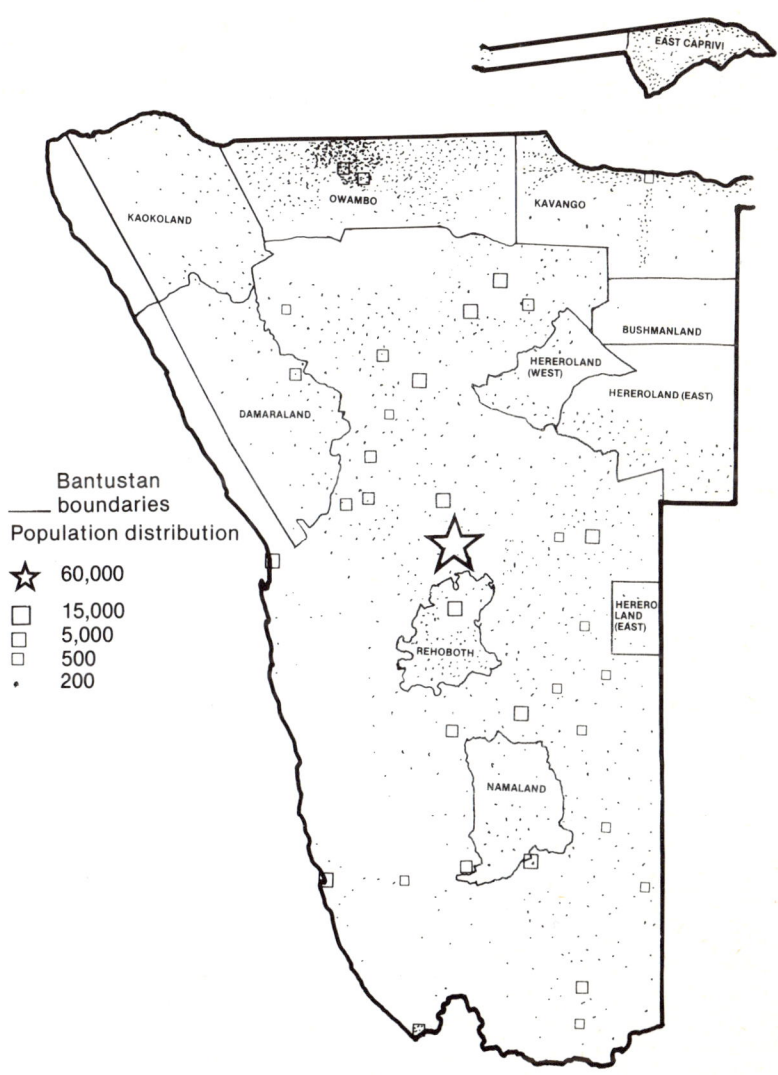

1 Education through Oppression

What is Education?

Education, in the broadest sense, is a lifelong process of learning: of searching for a better understanding of the world and learning to operate in it. Obviously, this booklet cannot hope to look at all such learning in Namibia. But to concentrate on the learning which takes place in schools, important as it is, would be too narrow. Instead, the emphasis here is on all those *institutions* in Namibian society (including organisations, customs and ways of communication) through which people learn.

Education in Pre-Colonial Namibia

In the early nineteenth century, the boundaries of present-day Namibia contained a variety of different communities. In the centre and south, where the climate was generally too dry for crops, there were three main types of society: small San (Bushman) hunting bands; Nama and Damara clans herding sheep and goats, and ranging from a few score to a couple of thousand people; and Herero cattle-pastoralists. By contrast, the Ovambo flood plain and the Okavango river valley in the north were fertile areas, where people lived in dense clusters of permanent settlement, separated by uninhabited woodland. The dozen clusters in Ovamboland were each politically independent, ranging in population from a thousand to 80 000. In the largest, hereditary rulers emerged; elsewhere, however, political authority was decentralised.

Although there were variations between different indigenous communities, education in pre-colonial Namibia was generally part of everyday life. It was not the responsibility of a specialist labour force called teachers (except, perhaps, the elderly). Rather, every adult had the responsibility, almost equal to that of the parents, to teach, correct, or even punish any child.

The roles and skills of adult society were learned through stories, riddles, poetry, and memory tests, as well as through traditions of song, dance and games. Transition to adult status was often accompanied by initiation ceremonies, stressing attitudes of solidarity and cooperation. In the main, the differentiation of adult roles was along sexual lines. Skills were often passed from father to son or from mother to daughter. Special skills such as blacksmithing, pot making, or healing, were generally monopolised by particular clans and passed on by the apprenticeship of younger members of the family.

The achievements of traditional 'African' education are impressive in terms of socal cohesiveness, the transmission of many useful skills, and the creation of a sense of history and identity. By experiment and observation Namibians developed skills suited to their circumstances; but innovation was undoubtedly confined by illiteracy and superstition.

Much of value in African cultures has been destroyed or lost; but it is also true that many values and ways of communication persist. Some should have a place in building the future, while other values are changing. Women especially are rejecting any subjugation. Similarly, Namibians want to foster a national identity, rather than the narrower tribal feeling which was the basis for social solidarity in the past[1].

Missionary Education

The first Europeans to settle in Namibia were traders and missionaries, and in particular the Rhenish Mission Society (RMS) of Germany, which arrived in 1842. Education played a central role in securing the spread of missions. Indigenous leaders saw missionary schooling as an opening to trade, improved technology and defence of their kingdoms. The missionaries preferred preaching to teaching, but schools at least gave them an acceptable role in the African communities. An unspoken bargain was struck, and mission education expanded.

By 1866 there was sufficient demand for schooling for the RMS to open a teacher training centre at Otjimbingwe in Western Namibia. Lutheran missionary activity expanded in 1870 when the Finnish Mission Society began work in the more densely populated northern

---

1. Blakemore and Cooksey 1981, p.11f; Mbamba 1982, p.31.

areas of Namibia. (The Anglican and Catholic Churches did not engage in much mission work until after the First World War).

If one goal of missionary education was to gain a foot in the door and establish Christian communities, there also was a deeper rationale: the imposition of a new social order. Missionaries were convinced that European values and civilisation were superior to African, and that it was their Christian calling to impart Western culture. As African chiefs generally rejected the missionaries' approaches, converts had to leave their people and take part in the formation of a new community on the mission stations, some of which were even called mission colonies. In the same vein, it was expected of blacks who joined the mission that they should become employees and artisans, able to participate in a capitalist economy. Training in practical skills and domestic service was accordingly introduced. A missionary by the name of Hoeflich summarised the objectives of missionary education in Namibia as follows:

> For its development . . . the country does not need 'educated Negros', but competent, intelligent workers. The main emphasis will therefore be on education for obedience, order, punctuality, sobriety, honesty, diligence, and moderation, rather than academic learning[2].

However, many white settlers in Namibia saw any eduction of blacks as a threat to colonisation.

Colonisation

The Namib and Kalahari deserts kept colonisers at bay until 1878. Even then, the British took possession only of Walvis Bay, the deep water port in Namibia. This tentative step disappointed the German missionaries, who looked increasingly to Germany as a potential colonial power. They intensified their efforts after conflict broke out in 1880 between the two main indigenous groups of central Namibia, the Nama and the Herero.

German colonisation of Namibia was initiated by the merchant Adolf Lüderitz, who hoped to gain wealth through the discovery of minerals.

Lüderitz actually bought two tracts of land, for the grand total of £600 and 260 rifles. With the assistance of missionaries, he established 'protection treaties' over large parts of southern and central Namibia, playing off one group against another, sometimes acquiring rights

---

2. Melber 1979, p.20.

from those who did not own them. Chiefs agreed to protect the life and property of Germans, who could trade freely, and promised not to enter into treaties with other nations. German rule was at first indirect: the German authorities retained control over their nationals, while recognising the jurisdiction of the chief over his people. In April 1884, having taken over Lüderitz's treaties, Bismarck was able to proclaim a German protectorate over parts of Namibia.

Despite Lüderitz's hopes, profitable deposits of minerals were not immediately discovered in the new colony. Instead more white settlers arrived. They engaged either in trade — using German protection for extortion of large profits — or cattle farming, encroaching on the grazing of Herero and Nama herds.

Under this increasing pressure, Namibians mounted a series of rebellions against the Germans, the most significant being the Herero and Nama rebellions of 1904-07. The Germans responded with fanatical nationalism, culminating in an attempt to exterminate the Herero, whose numbers were reduced, it has been estimated, from 70 000 to 15 000. This act of genocide overshadowed the dispossession of all Herero and Nama lands and cattle.

Despite their complicity with the German colonialists, missionaries were not killed in the rebellions, on the express orders of the Herero chiefs. However, the mission societies vigorously condemned the rebels, and continued to do so even when the survivors were made indentured labourers or put in mission care on inadequate reserves. Several missionaries inside Namibia did however contradict their mission superiors and sought to draw attention to the plight of black Namibians.

The missionaries, in this context, did not have a settled or successful time. But, if anything, the importance of education increased as blacks began to see education as one part of their struggle to regain their land. But the settlers feared education of blacks: it was not in their interest to have literate and numerate workers, and their own livelihoods as farmers, traders and artisans would be threatened by skilled blacks. The German government voted funds for black education, under pressure from liberals and socialists, but little was actually spent. In 1912 there were only some 5 500 black Namibians in school[3].

South Africa Takes Over

During the First World War, South Africa invaded Namibia on behalf of Britain and defeated the German garrison. South Africa had hoped

---

3. Melber 1979, p.30.

South African Schooltexts for Namibia: WARLIKE BLACKS AND PEACEFUL WHITES

The images in the texts reinforce a perception of whites as peaceful, resourceful and courageous and of blacks as warlike and ungrateful.

Source: 'History, Standard 3': Jordaan & Jordaan (1983); 'History 4': Lambrechts, Van Schoor, Bester & Potgieter (1980); 'History in Perspective Junior Standard 5': Broodryk & Lategan (1975)

The fact that the government of the Cape was prepared to protect the Black people from the Whites was more than the Voortrekkers could bear. The poor protection that they had received from the British government against the Black people had been one of the causes of the Great Trek.

The Battle of Vechtkop.

The Hottentots were angry because the Whites had taken their grazing grounds away from them. They did not wish to exchange their cattle for goods that the Whites offered them and began to steal from the Whites. This problem became so serious that van Riebeeck decided to send an expedition out against the Kaapman Hottentots and punish them. This was the first Hottentot war.

Dirkie Uys tries to save his wounded father.

The captains of the indigenous people were all *consulted* before the area was annexed. The Hereros were very pleased with the arrangements and 59 captains and headmen signed the agreement in 1876 on behalf of the Hereros.

Bushmen attacking a frontier farmer's house.

to annex Namibia as a fifth province, but instead the League of Nations placed Namibia under a 'C' mandate administered by South Africa. The intention of this kind of mandate was that the administering power should not benefit economically or militarily, but should develop the territory so that the inhabitants could determine their own future.

In practice, however, the new government used Namibia as a place to settle 'poor whites' being displaced from agriculture in South Africa. The division of land between white and black areas was confirmed and reinforced. At the same time, mining activity increased especially at the German-owned Tsumeb mine and the rich diamond fields which in 1919 were acquired by the South African Anglo-American Corporation.

For both white farms and mines, labour was needed. With the population of central Namibia decimated by the German campaigns, northern Namibia was the obvious source. Headmen were rewarded for each of their subjects who agreed to such work in the south of the country. The lack of alternatives for earning cash drove men south.

Education up to 1950

1. Education for blacks

Like the Germans, the South African administration wished to control, but not improve, missionary education of blacks. At a 1923 meeting with all missions, except the Finnish, it imposed a normal course of schooling of not longer than four years (up to standard two). The curriculum was restricted to reading, writing, arithmetic, religion and singing, all in the vernacular[4]. Nevertheless, by the 1930s the South African administration had become apprehensive about the educational work of the churches, severely limited as it was.

Of particular concern to South African officials was the 'bush school' movement. The Finnish Mission had published a first literacy primer in 1876. Because literacy was required for baptism, it developed a simple system for expanding the literate population. Everyone who had learnt to read had to teach others. The 'schools' would meet under a tree every weekday, and the 'teachers' would meet on a Saturday to discuss the lessons for the coming week. In 1913 a teacher training college was opened at Oniipa, and boarding schools started in the 1920s[5]. In 1924 there were reported to be 4 689 pupils in northern Namibia[6].

---

4. Ibid, p.23.
5. Shejavali 1970 and information provided by R. Voipio.
6. Melber 1979, p.31.

However, the 'Native Commissioner' Major Hahn did not approve of a system of education which could expand at a steady rate and teach the basics to large numbers of people at little expense. From 1932 onwards permission had to be obtained for each new school opened. In 1936 he conducted an inspection and ordered the closure of 84 out of 164 schools of the Finnish Mission[7]. However, the South African presence was, at that time, too weak in the north to enforce the closures, and Hahn's orders were largely ignored. In its 1936 report to the League of Nations, the South African government criticised the schools in northern Namibia for their poor standards and lack of facilities. However, the authorities made their real intentions clear by their refusal to make any more funds available for African education.

Between 1935 and 1956 seven state schools were opened in Herero reserves. This was probably because the German missions were too impoverished to undertake any additional work, and as a result of pressure from the League of Nations. In 1943 the South African government took over the Augustineum Teachers Training College, then in Okahandja, as the Second World War brought further financial difficulties for the Rhenish Mission Society. For the rest, Africans were dependent on missionaries, whose resources were painfully limited. The total black school population by 1945 was only 19 167 pupils[8].

There was no secondary education at all, and almost none in the higher primary grades. This was intensely frustrating for blacks.

2. Criticism by black people

There were several criticisms from black people of the education they received up to about 1950. As one spokesman put it:

> The greatest problem we must constantly touch on is the deplorable education that the youth enjoy. It is so limited that we do not see the necessity for letting it continue. The Missionary Schools, particularly those of the Rhenish Mission, prepare our youths only as hewers of wood, drawers of water and good kitchen hands. After our efforts in everything failed to achieve the desired results, we decided to take our children out of the hands of the above-mentioned Mission and to struggle further independently until such time as the government realises its duties towards us, and intervenes with its help. We have, however, no means of providing education but this is the only solution we can see for the advancement of our race. Knowing we are persecuted, put in gaol, and accused of distorting

---

7. Information provided by R. Voipio.
8. Melber 1979, p.31.

facts, we still cannot strike back because we seek nothing but education and development[9].

Other criticisms concerned the syllabus. One teacher of the Herero community pointed out that when they still had lands, people used to grow mealies, corn, watermelons, tobacco, kalabash, beans, and so on. He wanted the young to be trained in agriculture. Some objected to the concentration on religion, seeing it as a stifling indoctrination, though many early nationalist leaders drew their strength and inspiration from the Gospels[10].

3. Education for the settlers

During the German period, state schools were provided for the settlers, to ensure the maintenance of German culture. Even so, the German colonial government was not very generous and it has been estimated that only 21% of school-age settler children were in school when South Africa took over[11]. One apparently horrified German reported from a farm school:

> There are children of between 16 and 18 years coming to this school who can only read and write and count to ten with difficulty . . . The children will not sit on the benches, but prefer to sit on their haunches as they have learnt from the natives[12].

One of the first steps taken by the new South African government (proclamation 55 of 1921) was to make education compulsory for white children between the ages of 7 and 17.

However, fearing that the German settlers would collude with their fatherland for the recapture of Namibia, the South African government sought to discourage the use of German as a medium of instruction in the schools. White schools thus became an arena for conflict within Namibia.

South Africa set about imposing the 'Cape Syllabus' modelled on the British system. Whites could obtain primary and secondary education in Namibia, but for teacher training, vocational training and university studies they had to go to South Africa. Afrikaans and English were used as the medium of instruction in most state schools. The result was that most German children (the majority of the white population then) were put into private German-medium schools. Ironically (in view of the neglect of black education), when the

9. Troup 1950, p.216.
10. Scott 1955, p.225.
11. Melber 1979, pp.18 & 41.
12. Ibid, p.16.

government withdrew its subsidy of private schools, German nationalists charged that this denial of education was contrary to the League of Nations mandate! By the fifties, however, German was accepted in white schools, as the South African government tried to unite the different settler factions.

4. Education for coloureds

Another early step by South Africa (proclamation 16 of 1926) was to establish a separate education system for 'coloured' people, or those of 'mixed race', including the Basters who had settled at Rehoboth in the 1870s. Coloureds were not prevented from studying beyond standard 2, as was the case with black students; their syllabus was similar to that of the whites. On the other hand, the resources available for coloureds were little more than those for blacks. The intention was apparently that some semi-skilled manual workers should be filtered out for the service of the white-controlled economy[13].

Apartheid and its expression in education 1948-1977

Since its incorporation into the British Empire, South Africa was characterised by tensions between settlers of Dutch (Afrikaner) and English descent. Education became a key battleground. After the Boer War, the victorious British saw a common education as a means of uniting the white population. Nationalist Afrikaners saw this as an attempt to anglicise them, and the Afrikaans language and Dutch Reformed Church became rallying points for their resistance. Many Afrikaner teachers saw in the schools an opportunity to protect their interests, both cultural and economic, from the British Empire on the one hand and the African majority on the other. Under the banner of 'Christian National Education', they fought successfully for the separate education of their children in their mother tongue and for the teaching of history as the unfolding of God's plan for the Afrikaner *volk*[14].

In 1948 the Afrikaner Nationalists were victorious in a white election and set about entrenching their policy of apartheid, reinforcing racial separation and domination by whites in all spheres of life. Christian National Education now became official policy for whites. For blacks, the government introduced Bantu Education. The concepts of Bantu Education were drawn from the work of

---

13. Ibid, p.38.
14. Moodie 1975.

> **South African Schooltexts for Namibia:**
> **CIVILISATION**
> South African values are strongly emphasised: a Eurocentric and fundamentalist Christian view of 'civlilisation', whose carriers are the whites.
> Source: 'History in Perspective; Junior Standard 5': Broodryk & Lategan (1975)

1. THE EVOLUTION OF MAN
1.1 Man as a hunter
The book of Genesis, the first book of the Bible, tells the story of man's creation thousands of years before the birth of Christ.

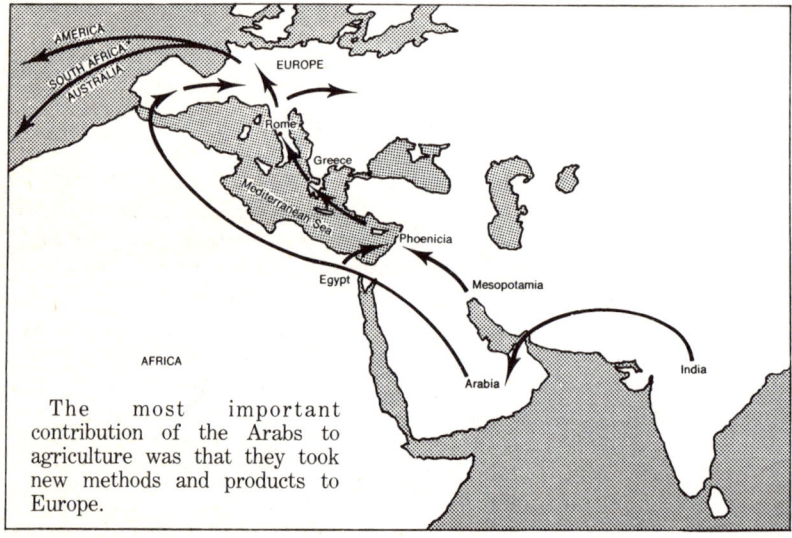

The most important contribution of the Arabs to agriculture was that they took new methods and products to Europe.

The spread of the alphabet and numerals

At the time of the Roman Empire (or civilisation), all those things that had come into being among the old civilisations were taken to the countries of Western Europe — to Britain, Holland, Germany, France, and so on. Thus it came about that our Western civilisation grew out of the old civilisations. When the fathers of our country, South Africa, settled here, they brought all these elements of civilisation from Europe.

the Eiselen Commission, appointed to devise a new system of black education in South Africa. It reported, contrary to racist ideology, that black children could do as well as their white counterparts in academic tests. If blacks were to remain subordinate, their education must, by implication, be limited. On the other hand, Eiselen was faced with the problem that South Africa would need large numbers of literate blacks for its booming industrial economy. The Commission resolved the dilemma by recommending that the emphasis should fall on providing a four-year primary education aimed at literacy and a utilitarian knowledge of English and Afrikaans 'to be used in contacts with the European sector of the population'. The remainder of the syllabus should create an interest in tribal heritage, agriculture, religion and hygiene[15].

The government's intention was made plain by the architect of Bantu Education (and much other apartheid doctrine), Dr Verwoerd:

> There is no place for the native in the European community, above the level of certain forms of labour . . . Until now he has been subjected to a school system which drew him away from his own community and misled him by showing him the green pastures of European society in which he was not allowed to graze. . . When I have control of native education I will reform it so that the natives will be taught from childhood to realise that equality with Europeans is not for them . . . People who believe in equality are not desirable teachers for natives[16].

The recommendations of the Eiselen Commission were made law in South Africa by the Bantu Education Act of 1953.

These South African policies of course had an echo in Namibia. The Bantu Education Act was not immediately made applicable, probably because of United Nations concern over South African abuses in its administration of Namibia. However, from 1955, administrative powers were used to introduce what amounted to Bantu Education, and in 1958 the Van Zyl Commission was appointed to set up an education system for black and coloured Namibians.

Not surprisingly, the Commission found 'a striking similarity in the background of SWA natives and that of the Bantu of the Union (of South Africa)'. It recommended:
— the introduction of South Africa's Bantu education syllabus;
— the handing over of church schools to the state;
— an education levy on Africans; and
— the setting up of a separate education department for Africans

---

15. O'Callaghan 1977, p.99f; Melber 1979, p.67f.
16. Melber 1979, p.68f.

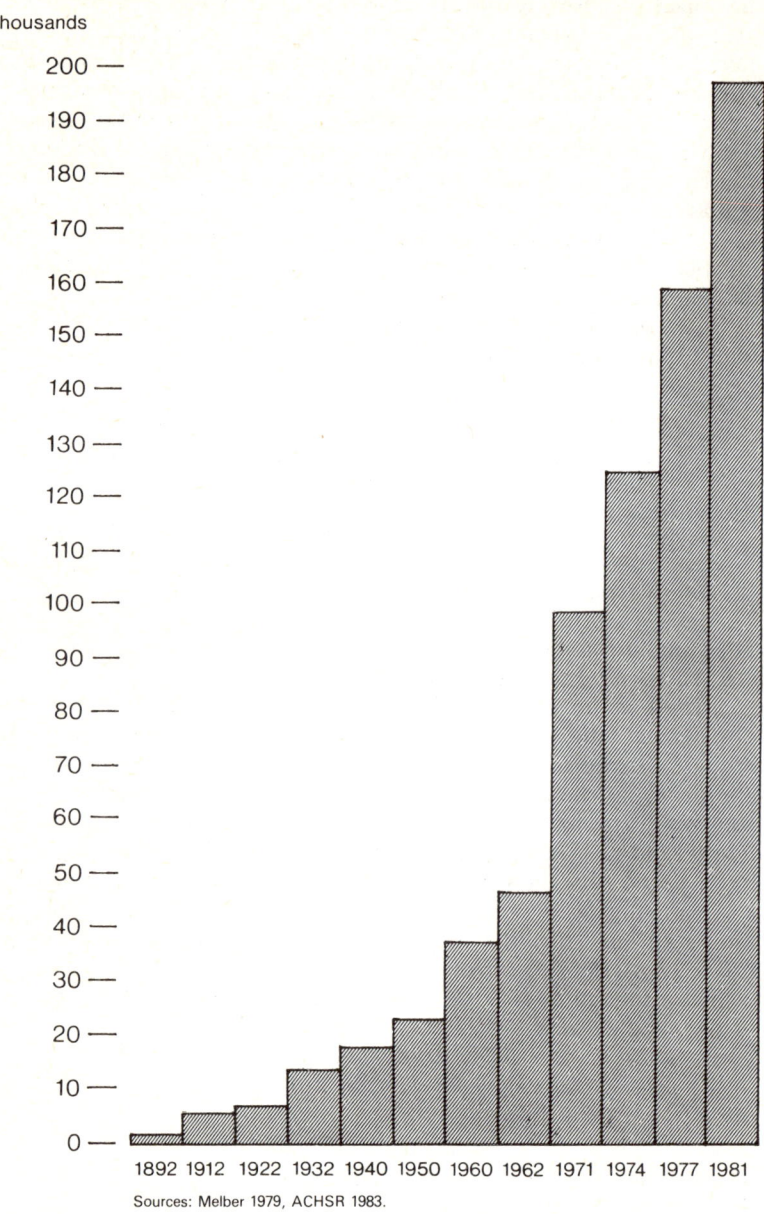

Figure 1. Number of students in black schools 1892-1981

Sources: Melber 1979, ACHSR 1983.

including a Language Bureau which should be headed by a white.
There were essentially three components to the plan. First, the number of blacks with a four year (lower primary) education was to be increased. The target would be to provide 80% of black school-age children with 4 years of primary education by 1988 — a considerable, if slow, expansion. The expansion was in line with the belief that white employers needed literate workers. Black education was also required to transmit the ideology of 'separate development' and to produce staff for the lower echelons of government.

Second, black education was to be moved from the churches to the state. In part this was because the meagre resources of the churches could not pay for the planned expansion of education. But the churches also could not be trusted to teach the new syllabus with the right emphasis. Opposition to apartheid was strengthening in the churches, and Namibians were petitioning the UN Trusteeship Council through channels opened by Anglican Rev Michael Scott.

The third component of the Van Zyl Commission's plan was that education beyond the lower primary level was to be severely restricted. Only 20% of those completing this 4 year cycle would go on to a higher primary school. In line with the government's policy of emphasising differences between ethnic groups, one secondary school was to be provided for each tribal group. Education up to matriculation (university entrance) level was to be provided for blacks in only two high schools, serving all tribal groups in the country[17].

The Education Ordinance of 1962 empowered Dr Van Zyl, as the head of African education, to carry out these plans. The strategy was endorsed by the wider Odendaal Commission of 1964, which drew up a blueprint for the establishment of Bantustans or separate ethnic states in Namibia, each to have its own impoverished administration, including a department of education.

The deliberate suppression of black secondary and even higher primary education dovetailed with South African plans for Namibia. Propaganda could be made at the World Court and elsewhere that by expanding primary education South Africa was supporting 'mass education' (then a fashionable term). The very explicit intention of Bantu Education was that blacks should be confined to the lowest grades, with their ambitions restricted to a tribal context. Yet this was apparently one of the main triggers for the assertion of new nationalist protest and political organisation. The leaders of this new political movement in Namibia during the late fifties and early sixties were often those blacks who had managed to obtain some education but

---

17. O'Callaghan 1977, pp.104-109; Melber 1979, pp.87-89.

then found their way blocked. In the few higher institutions, such as the Augustineum College, students debated ideas and built up a sense of national identity.

Their entry into political opposition was met with vicious oppression, an experience which soon led them to make common cause with the rising protests of migrant workers. The authorities in Namibia had left no 'escape hatch' for ambitious individuals. The result was a united nationalist movement.

An experience of this kind is recorded in the autobiography of John Ya Otto:

> In 1956 and 1957 the papers were full of articles about the bus boycott and other protests against the government in South Africa. In 1957 Ghana became independent under Kwame Nkrumah, an educated and articulate man who was respected by many Europeans but whom our teachers considered as just another Kaffir who would ruin everything the British had done to build up his country . . .
>
> One day, shortly after the 1957 winter break, Efraim Mieze showed me a leaflet he had brought back from South Africa . . . it described how the whites of South Africa's ruling Nationalist party saw themselves as the *Herrenvolk*, the master race, how they exploited black people, how their police beat and harassed us . . .
>
> The crumpled sheet felt like fire in my hands; we'd be in trouble if somebody caught us with this . . .
>
> Though I did my best, I could not block out of my mind what I had read in the leaflet. Everywhere I turned troublesome questions turned up. My favourite subject in school was history, but our textbook contradicted the stories every Namibian child is told by the elders. The Germans had never been 'invited by warring tribes' to bring peace to our country, neither had South Africa brought us prosperity. True, we had fought among ourselves, and the Germans had taken advantage of this to conquer us all. The text, however, said nothing about our grandparents' resistance, and about the terrible slaughter of the Hereros and Namas that followed the conquest. Even as late as the 1930s, air force planes had bombed Chief Ipumbu's village at Ukwambi, not far away from my birthplace . . .
>
> The years at Augustineum had taught me this: if we Africans wanted to learn, we would have to rely on ourselves[18].

Ya Otto became a teacher in Windhoek. He participated in the boycott of municipal facilities in 1959 which resulted in the massacre of protesters, and was an organiser of SWAPO inside Namibia for many years, eventually fleeing the country in 1974, to become SWAPO Secretary for Labour.

---

18.   Ya-Otto, 1982, p.29f.

Namibia since 1971

In 1966, the United Nations formally withdrew South Africa's mandate to govern Namibia. In 1971, the International Court of Justice confirmed that South Africa's continued occupation was illegal. In the same year, a great strike broke out across the mines and towns of Namibia, partly organised by students who had been expelled from state schools for demonstrating in support of the World Court ruling. The strike was directed against the migrant labour system, the 'contract' or 'wire' as it was called; at least half the migrant labour force returned to their rural homes, demanding an end to 'contract'. The strike ended when the South African administration conceded a new system of recruitment. The effect of these two events, one external and one internal, reverberated through the 1970s, bringing change and confrontation throughout the society, including education. Transnational companies, white farmers, black farmers and workers and the South African administration itself each reacted differently.

Most immediately affected were the transnational mining companies. The legal position, especially of new mines, was extremely weak. The UN Security Council followed the 1971 International Court of Justice ruling with a resolution declaring that states could not protect their companies from the claims of a future independent government in Namibia over rights issued by South Africa after the end of the mandate. New mines have nevertheless been opened, including Rössing Uranium. Companies have realised, however, the importance of projecting a favourable image, and of trying to build a body of support for their continued operations in the country after independence. This has been the motivation for the transnationals' support for black education, especially for higher education producing potential managers and skilled personnel. Consolidated Diamond Mines (de Beers) took the lead, with a R1½ million Valombola Technical Institute in Ovamboland (training artisans), and the R5 million Concordia College in Windhoek opened in 1983. This multi-racial college unashamedly aims to build up an elite through academic education; it starts at Form III, and total enrolment will increase from 500 to 1 800 over a few years[19]. CDM, Rössing and Tsumeb Corporation offer scholarships for degree and diploma students.

With much publicity, mining and commericial interests in Namibia have also established several foundations, such as the

---

19. *Windhoek Observer* 23 June 1979; *Windhoek Advertiser* 6 April 1982, 17 May 1982, 9 August 1982.

Rössing Foundation, the *Private Sector Foundation* and the *CDM Chairman's Fund*. These are setting up adult education and community programmes, the most visible of which is the Rössing Foundation adult education centre, built on the outskirts of the coloured township in Windhoek. The centre mostly provides language courses in English, Afrikaans and German. A workshop was added in 1983. The combined impact of these projects is not large in proportion to the size of population, but they gain attention for the companies.

At the same time as mining companies were initiating these projects, their own labour needs were changing. The 1971 strike caused a rise in wages, and also brought home to management the dissatisfaction of the workers and the potential damage they could cause. One of the principal causes of dissatisfaction was (and remains) restricted promotion opportunities for black workers. Meanwhile, the late 1970s saw an acute shortage of artisans throughout southern Africa — skilled white workers became both harder and more expensive to recruit. Continuing mechanisation also meant that money could be saved in some operations by replacing skilled workers by semi-skilled.

From the mid-1970s onwards, these factors within the mining companies led to a new emphasis on training black workers. In the early 1970s, Tsumeb and CDM began to train blacks for semi-skilled jobs previously reserved for whites. These developed, as at Rössing, into full-scale upgrading programmes. In the late 1970s, these three principal companies admitted their first black apprentices. This training has had considerable effect at the semi-skilled level; much less change has occurred at skilled and especially professional levels[20].

If mining companies were putting pressure on the administration for increased secondary and technical education, the white farming community had no such concerns. Here training remains unimportant. If anything, there has been a trend towards casual rather than permanent labour[21], and, in the present economic crisis, anything which raises wages would meet a hostile response. It may perhaps be in part the residual political strength of the white ranching community which accounts for the tardiness of the administration in pressing ahead with such secondary and technical education.

For black Namibians, whether small farmers (generally women), migrant workers (generally men) or those living in the townships, education has assumed an ever greater importance as a potential escape-route from poverty. The overcrowded farming areas of the north have become progressively less able to support the population

---

20. CIIR 1983, pp.74-77.
21. Moorsom 1983, p.33.

— in 1974, only a third of household income came from the land. In the central and southern stock-farming bantustans, six successive years of drought have combined with overcrowding to decimate herds and flocks[22]. Waged jobs are seen as the way out, and jobs increasingly require at least a basic education. Education of one's children may also be a form of investment for old age: educated children will probably earn more and so be better able to care for their parents in later life.

Parents' efforts to obtain education for their children can also be seen as part of a rejection of the present political order. It is an attempt to obtain, by sacrifice, what the government is trying to deny — the right to a job and a status on equal terms with whites. It can even be seen as an endorsement of educated leaders, such as those in the liberation movement, and a rejection of the kind of leadership provided by some unschooled headmen, used in the past by South Africa as its stooges.

Yet in striving for the education of their children, parents face a painful paradox. Though all must pay for education, only a few children reach secondary school. There is always a cost, such as school uniforms and the loss of children's contribution to household duties. In order to pay for schooling, people must go 'on contract' as migrant labourers more often; they must sell their cattle and handicrafts. Great sacrifices are made, but few succeed.

Political changes

South Africa, as occupying power, could not remain unmoved by the mounting internal and external pressures in the 1970s. In 1977 South Africa gave all power in the territory to an Administrator General who was appointed, ostensibly, to cooperate with the United Nations in the decolonisation of Namibia. Despite elaborate plans for elections, the Administrator General has not used his powers to decolonise Namibia. Instead, he has tried to foster a political alliance including some black figures, which depends on South African support but is presentable internationally as 'multiracial'. The objective is to create an 'independence settlement' excluding SWAPO. In case this strategy fails, South Africa also has a fall-back programme. This entails establishing a black Namibian elite in privileged positions and so giving them an interest in resisting attempts by any future SWAPO government to change existing institutions.

There is therefore a serious attempt by the South Africans to promote a small but significant black middle class. It goes alongside the recruitment of small numbers of blacks into skilled and

---

22. Ibid, pp.45-61.

management trainee positions in transnational companies; a handful of prominent black people have also been appointed to the Boards of Directors of local companies. Another group have managed to establish themselves, through corruption as well as legal salaries, in the various ethnic administrations of the bantustans: to the horror of its own civil servants, South Africa has, to date, allowed virtually unlimited expenditure.

A third group in this potential new middle class are teachers. It is in this context that one of the most important changes since 1978 in the education field has been improvement in teachers' salaries and housing conditions. The increments affect principals and matriculants especially, who now earn the same as their overpaid white counterparts (see Table 7). The government has also promoted a teachers' association which brings together various ethnic teachers' associations but is dominated by whites. The association concentrates on conditions of employment, avoiding discussion of social policies. The objective of these measures is obviously to obtain the collaboration, or at least the quiescence, of black teachers. Government agents now put it about that such and such a teacher cannot support the socialist principles of the liberation movement, considering the car he has just bought, the extension he is making to his house, and the domestic servant he hires. It would be a mistake however to assume that teachers have in fact been swung to favour South Africa; the most serious long term effect is likely to be on their expectations for their own standard of living after independence.

Through successive Administrators General, South Africa has created a three-tier structure of government in Namibia: municipalities, ethnic governments and central government. At the municipal level, black townships are still effectively ruled by city councils, elected by whites ten years ago. But wealthy blacks can now buy houses in desirable suburbs, previously reserved for whites. The government has also started housing programmes which enable middle class blacks (such as teachers) to obtain reasonable housing.

The second level consists of eleven ethnic governments. Each ethnic government is responsible for the primary and secondary education of a particular population or language group as defined by the government. Other functions, such as health and agriculture, also come under second-tier governments. The effect of these ethnic divisions is to perpetuate segregation and inequalities, as the whites maintain their privileged schools, hospitals, commercial licences and subsidies for farming. Several of the ethnic governments have been unable to take responsibility for education, and have ceded it to the central government. Generally the ethnic governments have been a fertile bed for corruption, as has become apparent through the recent

Thirion Commission into mismanagement of state funds. The official 1983 Report to the Department of National Education by the Advisory Committee for Human Sciences Research (ACHSR) admits that ethnic authorities 'can hardly administer their education systems'[23]. Educational expenditure is said to have increased by 45% since 1981/82, but the Report says that the ethnic governments are apparently redirecting these resources to fields other than education, as they are legally entitled to do[24].

The central or third tier of government was meant to be drawn from the eleven ethnic governments — each ethnic government having a veto over central government — but this has collapsed. Instead the Administrator General has formed his own central authority, consisting of several committees which are dominated by representatives of the South African military and some from business.

Central government has authority over post-secondary education. A department of National Education has been created, but in practice does not have the power to impose policy on any ethnic education department. The department absorbed the former Bantu Education officials. It has advertised for subject specialists, but so far has done very little to produce a curriculum which is Namibian rather than South African. According to the official ACHSR Report, the National Examination Board and the National Education Council — umbrella bodies legally constituted in 1980 — are powerless and ineffective, and educational support services, especially for curriculum development, language teaching, guidance and planning, do not exist or are inadequate[25].

In an attempt to gain popular support the 'ethnic administration' of Ovamboland, the most heavily populated area of Namibia, has introduced English as the medium of instruction in upper primary schools. Previously, the emphasis had been on Afrikaans, hated as the language of the oppressor and useless in the international community. Many teachers are doing their best to teach in English, but most lack the training or support programmes to do so effectively.

The introduction of the syllabus used in the Cape Province of South Africa for all schools in Namibia may also be looked upon as a concession; if qualified teachers are available, it could improve standards in mathematics and the sciences. However, it continues to promote white domination, and the emphasis is on South Africa rather than Namibia. The Geography textbook for Standard 4, for example, devotes no more space to Namibia than it does to Egypt[26].

---

23. Advisory Committee on Human Sciences Research 1983 Vol. 5, p.101.
24. Ibid, p.99
25. Ibid, p.85f.
26. Beyers, Knoetze and Preuss, *Geography 4*, Johannesburg 1982.

South African Schooltexts for Namibia:
WHITE INITIATIVE AND BLACK LABOUR

The civilising mission of the whites is presented in an unrepentently imperial fashion.

Source: 'History, Standard 2': Jordaan & Jordaan (1983); 'History 4': Lambrechts, Van Schoor, Bester & Potgieter (1980); 'History in Perspective, Standard 5': Broodryk & Lategan (1975); 'History, Standard 3': Jordaan & Jordaan (1983).

Labour
Another resource in which South Africa is very rich is labour. With our large population of all race groups we have a labour supply to support the development of our mines and industries. The relative absence of strikes and disputes is an indication that this labour force is very stable.

David Livingstone

Fig. 2.1 Van Riebeeck's landing at the Cape

Fig. 2.2 A postal messenger in early-day SWA

1.3.2 The slaves as labourers

Slaves were bought and sold at the slave market in Cape Town. They were valued according to their ability. Negroes were the cheapest and were good only for the most elementary work — farm work, gardening, and hard labour in general. Domestic slaves were of a better quality. The best, and most expensive, were slaves who had trained as artisans or craftsmen.

The best slaves at the Cape were the Malays. They came from the East Indies and were more developed than slaves from other parts. These Malay slaves were neat, intelligent, and competent. As artisans or craftsmen (cabinet makers, tailors, shoemakers, builders, musicians) they were very valuable.

In the course of time a group of cross-bred slaves (a Hottentot-slave mixture) came into being. These cross-breeds were good farm labourers and domestic servants.

In terms of Company law, cross-bred children were *booked* in with the owners of the parents. Owners had to see to their education.

1.3.3 How slaves were treated at the Cape.

Slaves at the Cape were reasonably well cared for — generally far better than in other parts of the world. There were exceptions, but on the whole they were well clothed and fed and humanely punished. The Company slaves were possibly worse off than the slaves at the Cape.

2 Education Today

Having reviewed some of the main aspects of the history of education in Namibia, we are now in a position to review the present state of education, both formal and informal. We begin with schooling.

During 1982, the total budget for all forms of state education in Namibia was roughly as in Table 6. Total allocations for education were about 12% of the national budget, excluding what was spent by South Africa on the war. By comparison, education expenditure in neighbouring Botswana was somewhat over 25% of recurrent expenditure[1].

Black Primary Education

The introduction of Bantu Education and its successors undoubtedly brought about a decline in the quality of education. The greater resources of the state (as compared to the churches) did bring about a rapid increase in enrolments. In fact they continue to increase far faster than predicted (the 1981/82 projected increase was 14 456, but 26 404 new enrolments were recorded according to the ACHSR report[2]). One consequence is very large classes: the ACHSR Report estimated that over 50% more classrooms would have been needed in 1981 to have allowed classes of 30 pupils[3]. Despite the increasing numbers of students, however, the objective of providing basic literacy was not achieved, because few school students stayed four to

---

1. Government of Botswana, Fifth National Development Plan (Gaborone, 1979).
2. Advisory Committee for Human Sciences Research (ACHSR) 1983 Vol. 5, p.102.
3. Ibid, p.101 for increase; Department of National Education Statistics 1980 for number in 1980.

Figure 2. Proportion of pupils in different classes 1981

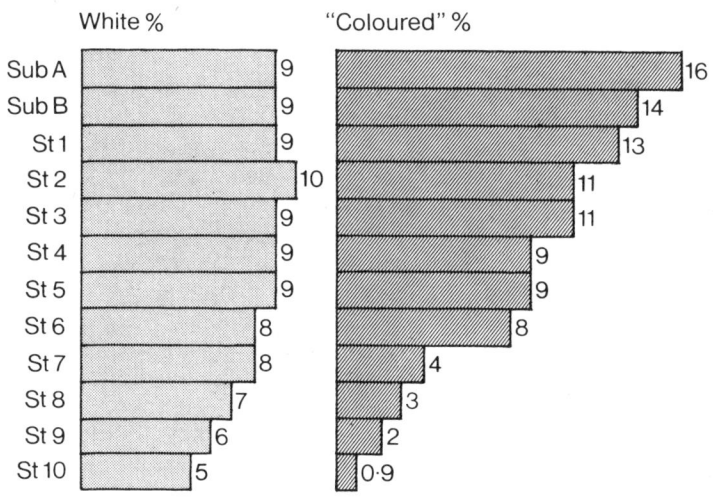
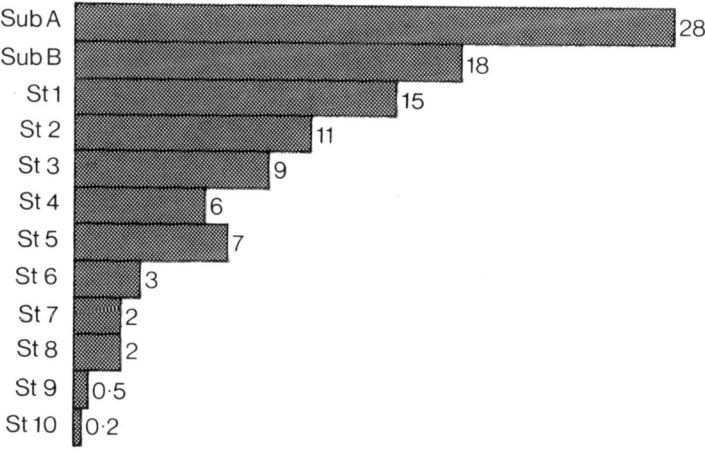

Notes
1. This shows the percentage of students in each class. For example, 9% of white students are in Sub A.
2. There was a total of 197 533 black students, 33 315 coloured and 18 171 white students.

Source: Table 1

six years in school. Sixty per cent of the population probably still are illiterate. The ACHSR Report admitted that at best only two-thirds of 1981 school leavers were functionally literate[4].

Most black children now go to school at some stage, even if only for a few months or years. Those who miss out completely are mostly on the white-owned farms or in isolated places like railway encampments. In 1982 the enrolment in black schools was probably just over 200 000, or about 16% of the black population. However, almost three-quarters (71%) of black pupils in 1980 were in lower primary schools. Only 22% of them were in upper primary schools, and a mere 7% in secondary and vocational training. These are astounding figures — considerably worse than comparable African countries (see Figure 2 and Tables 3 and 4).

Part of the explanation may be that education is being expanded, and new students have to enter at the beginners' classes. However, the main problems are firstly that a great many of those who start drop out after a very few years, and secondly that many children repeat years in the lower classes, rather than moving on. The ACHSR Report attaches particular importance to this, pointing out (Figure 3) that the number of students in Sub A (officially the first year of schooling intended for seven year old children) was more than double the number of seven year olds in the country. The reasons for the heavy drop-out rate and irregular attendance are fairly obvious:

— Many children and their families are too hungry to sacrifice resources of money, time and energy for the kind of education which is on offer. There are other tasks that children can do, such as herding animals or fetching water.
— Malnourished children cannot walk far or study well.
— Classes are large. The average size in 1980 was 37 pupils, but in the lower grades the classes are often double this size. The first class (Sub A) often has 100 pupils. Principals generally allocate trained staff to the higher standards.
— Most teachers are poorly trained. In 1980, 40% of teachers had a primary school certificate and some teacher training; another 40% had, at most, a junior secondary certificate, but no teacher training. The ACHSR Report admits[5] that three-quarters of Namibia's teachers have too little education themselves to provide high quality teaching (see Table 8). The motivation of some teachers is moreover very low because of their hostility towards the curriculum and the authorities.

---

4. ACHSR 1983, Vol. 5, p.71.
5. Ibid, p.80.

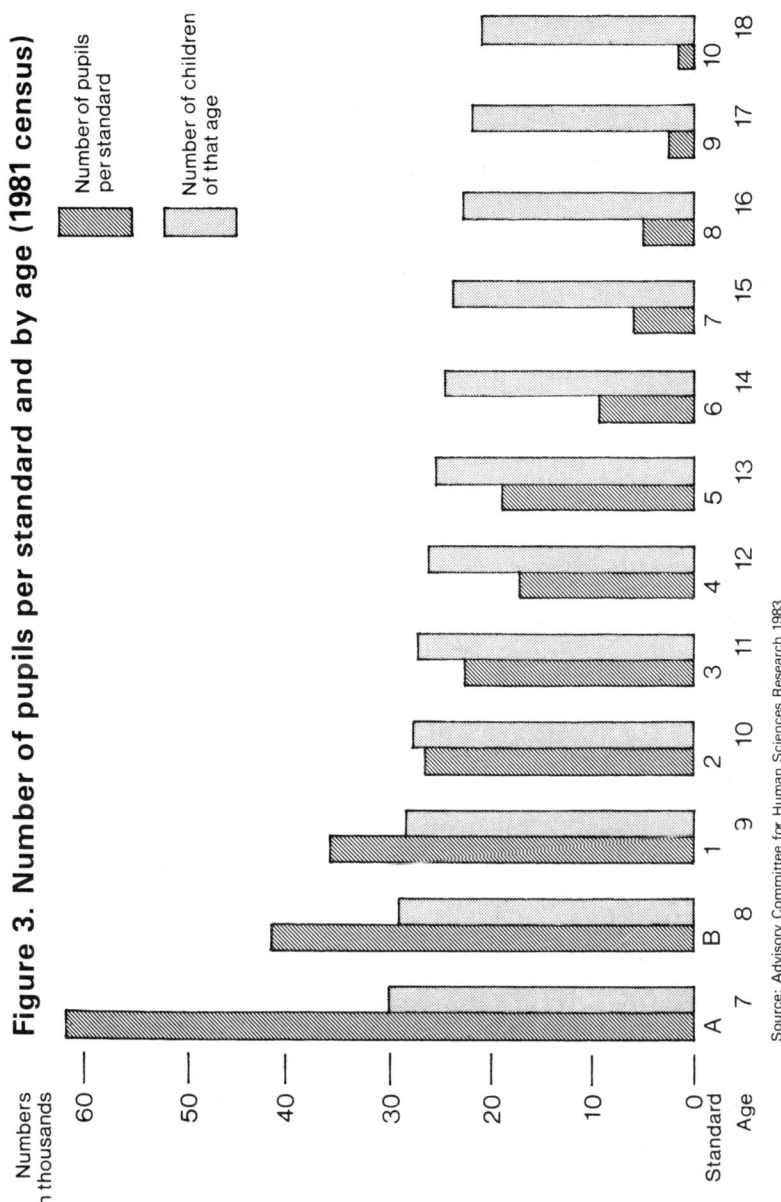

Figure 3. Number of pupils per standard and by age (1981 census)

Source: Advisory Committee for Human Sciences Research 1983

— The curriculum used in the schools is offensive to blacks, or at best, confusing.
— Conscription has driven many Namibians out of school, especially as the military authorities have used school registers to recruit.
— A primary school certificate is not necessarily 'rewarded' with escape from migrant labour, or access to secondary school and lucrative jobs.
— Rote learning and harsh discipline are the order of the day in most schools, which have insufficient books and equipment for work or play.
— Many children are under pressure to perform domestic duties (often with only one parent at home) or go out and find work themselves. They themselves soon realise that it is those — both black and white — who have money to pay the fees (especially for secondary school), to buy uniforms, books and domestic help who are going to complete their schooling.

Teachers at primary school experience many acute conflicts in their work. They have two masters. On the one hand they are entrusted with the hopes of parents; on the other, the South African government wants to use them as agents of the apartheid state. In an attempt to co-opt them, the government has increased teachers' salaries; but at the same time the occupying army in the north often suspects teachers of being SWAPO supporters.

These contradictions cannot easily be resolved by teachers. They know that they do not have the skills or equipment to cope with classes of 40 to 100 pupils. They do not like the syllabus. They must somehow make it clear to their communities that they do not approve of the racist government which provides them with their bread, knowing that if this 'open secret' catches the attention of the informers in their schools, they can be summarily dismissed, or detained by the army or security police. One result of this conflict is poor morale. Some teachers simply neglect their school work, doing the minimum that they can get away with.

Black Secondary Education

No secondary education was available to black Namibians before 1953, when the Augustineum College offered the first junior secondary course. Thirty-two candidates reached the third form in 1955, with the first three completing their studies in 1959. In Northern Namibia, secondary education began in 1961. It has largely depended on a handful of church schools and several showpiece state schools[6].

---

6. Melber 1979, pp.29 & 36.

More recently, partly under pressure from international mining companies and commercial interests, the South African government has begun to expand secondary and vocational education.

The total enrolment of blacks in secondary education is now in the region of 14 000. But very few successfully complete their schooling. In 1982, only 261 blacks obtained a school leaving certificate (std 10) compared to 131 coloureds and 832 whites. Of these only 23 blacks and 7 coloureds were granted University entrance, compared to 359 whites[7]. From 1983, however, numbers will be boosted by the opening of the Concordia College in Windhoek.

The ACHSR Report admits that the small flow of pupils to secondary school means that black and coloured pupils leave school with too little education to meet the increasing demand for skilled workers. Not more than 17% of all school-leavers, according to the Report, could be accepted for further training as skilled workers, and in particular poor performance at mathematics, science and technical drawing mean that a negligible number of pupils achieve a formal vocational qualification or recognised trade certificate[8].

Not surprisingly, Namibia's secondary schools have been places of conflict between young Namibians and the South African authorities. Virtually every year since 1971 there has been some outbreak of hostility, often ending in mass expulsions of pupils, the sacking of teachers and the victimisation, even torture, of supposed 'agitators'. One of the main causes of such conflict has been the government's attempt to impose its ideology through white head teachers in state schools. Recently many whites have withdrawn from black areas because of the guerilla war, and the South African army has increasingly placed armed white conscripts as teachers in schools.

The conflicts in secondary education have been a factor drawing many students into the liberation movement, with its radically different concept of education, leading them to abandon the pursuit of a certificate (the key to one of the few lucrative jobs open to blacks). One Namibian 'drop-out', who managed to spend some time at a South African black university, has described his experience:

> Under that system (Bantu Education) you are inhibited with fear and you are never free to ask anything. Nor are you taught everything, but only certain things . . .
>
> The South African universities are just factories for duplicating individualistic people, and most of the students come with this attitude of 'owning something for myself' . . .
>
> After receiving the degree you want to buy a big house, big car,

---

7. *Windhoek Observer* 24 December 1982.
8. ACHSR 1983, Vol. 5, p.71.

forgetting the people, even your parents at home. But back here, I realised that the struggle is for the people. And we can start off an education which we can call people's education . . .[9]

One result of the conflict in secondary education has been that two private schools have opted out of the official system and now teach the Botswana, Lesotho and Swaziland syllabus. The Martin Luther School in Okombahe and the private Gibeon community school (created after a teachers' strike) have, however, not found this an easy path. It has been difficult to achieve the necessary standard of English. The change from rote-learning to more critical thinking has imposed further demands. The syllabus remains, in part, foreign to Namibia, and those who succeed in passing the British-set examinations face discrimination from employers.

Technical education at secondary level has also been very restricted. In 1976 there were only 261 Africans being trained as carpenters, mechanics, builders, etc., and their training would not make them full artisans[10]. In 1980 this number had reached 380, with the opening of a new technical college, Valombola College (sponsored by CDM) at Ongwediva in Northern Namibia[11]. Agricultural training has been similarly neglected: the agricultural school at Ogongo in Ovamboland, one of only two for black Namibians, had only 20 trainees in 1982. By contrast, there were 60 trainees at the white agricultural college[12]. Almost all vocational training has been for boys or men. The main career openings for women are as social work assistants, teachers, or nurses.

Teacher-training under South African rule has fallen far short of needs. During 1976, 592 Africans were undergoing a two-year teacher training course — but only for primary school; there was no course for secondary school teachers[13]. In 1980, 547 teachers were in training, 31 as secondary school teachers[14]. The ACHSR Report points out that a maximum of 293 teachers may qualify in 1983, but 460 would be needed just to cater for the growth in school enrolments without allowing for replacement of retiring teachers. However, several hundred teachers are now being assisted to study part-time in government schemes and through the Academy for Tertiary Education[15].

---

9.   South African Labour Bulletin, 1978, p.73.
10. Melber 1979, p.191.
11. Department of National Education Statistics 1980. Valombola can accomodate 150 students. *Windhoek Advertiser* 20 May 1983.
12. Moorsom 1983, p.71.
13. Melber 1979, p.193.
14. Department of National Education Statistics 1980.
15. ACHSR Vol. 5 1983, p.82.

White Education

The difference between white education and black education lies not in the syllabus (which is equally prejudiced) but in the resources devoted to whites (see Fig.4 and Table 5).

Figure 4. 1981 Education expenditure per pupil

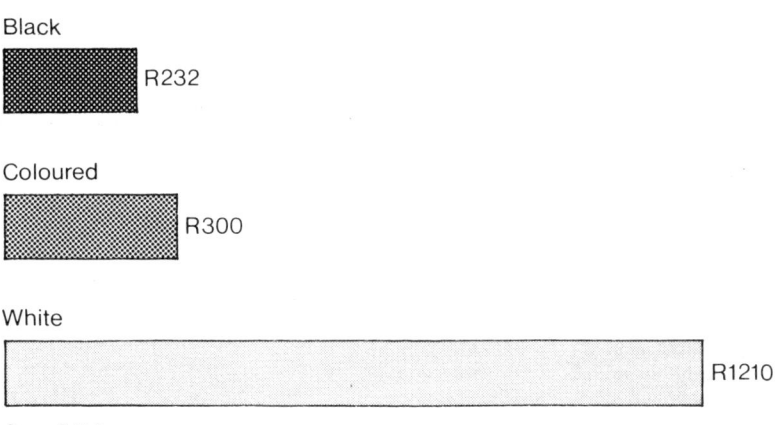

Source: Table 6.

    The provision of ten years' compulsory and segregated education for whites is an expensive enterprise. Education for whites (about 5-7% of the population) costs almost half of the amount spent on black education. In part, this is because many whites may choose English, Afrikaans or German medium schools. Many hostels are maintained to cater for a thinly-spread population. As white South Africans flee at the prospect of independence, school rolls are falling without costs being cut significantly. The pupil-teacher ratio in 1981 was 13:1. Some white schools have been closed, but, of course, are not made available for black education.
    White children are also forced into several militaristic activities, including cadet corps and holiday camps where instruction in bush skills is mingled with propaganda about 'the total onslaught' against South Africa.
    Private schools run by the Churches are now 'open', and a steadily increasing number of black and coloured families can now afford the fees.

South African Schooltexts for Namibia: CIVILISATION UNDER SIEGE

Training for citizenship inculcates a sense of a civilisation under siege.

Source: 'History 4': Lambrechts, Van Schoor, Bester & Potgieter (1980)

C. Citizenship

In Std 3 you were introduced to the rights and privileges of a citizen of the country. Apart from the duties and responsibilities imposed on a citizen by the state there are certain qualities within the person that have to be developed in order for him to become a useful citizen.

Patriotism

We are privileged to be able to live in a sunny land which is rich in raw materials and has the potential to produce enough food to feed its own inhabitants. Futhermore, the country offers opportunities of employment to all who are prepared to do hard and honest work.

This fatherland of ours was tamed by our hardy forefathers and built up into the prosperous land which it is today. This was no easy task. Earlier this year you learnt about the Voortrekkers and their privations. We also saw how Natal, the Orange Free State and the Transvaal had to struggle for their independence and how after that union was brought about and how the republican ideal was realised in 1961.

In the fields of agriculture, mining and industry, great achievements have been made. Hard work, courage and determination are required from everyone if we wish to continue on this path of development, and if we in the present world-situation wish to make this country a safe and happy place for its inhabitants.

Threats from the outside world, the danger of communism and terrorism force us to unite and be prepared to face up to any threat or danger.

What can you do, as a citizen, to make a positive contribution to the welfare of your country?. It is the duty of each pupil to enjoy the privilege of attending school to prepare him — or herself as well as possible for his or her vocation.

Our land needs the best-qualified people. All the qualities of a useful citizen as studied in Std 3 should become part of your life to ensure that your country can depend on you.

In the military field as well, your country directs an appeal to you. When our country is threatened, our safety is at stake. Every boy should strive to make the safety and survival of his country one of his personal responsibilities. That is why every boy must take part in the defence of his country and undergo military training.

To love your country means to be prepared to make sacrifices for it when it requires them.

At thy will to live or perish,
O South Africa, dear land.

Everyone should know how to act in the event of a disaster.
There are also man-made disasters such as accidents, fires and riots which cause the province and its inhabitants great inconvenience.

Activities

1. Why should we love our country?
2. What can I do to prove my love for my country?
3. Why is religion of such importance in one's life?
4. What does it mean to have a sense of values?

Coloured Education

In 'coloured' education, we are again faced with a misnomer as three unequal education departments fall under coloured education: those for Rehobothers, Coloureds and Namas.

The government has been more generous to coloured education than black, allowing about 30% more cash for each coloured schoolchild than for their black counterparts. The intention has been not just to create divisions between different oppressed groups, but to 'produce' some semi-skilled and skilled artisans who can do those jobs for which insufficient whites are available. As coloureds (with some exceptions) already have Afrikaans as their home language, this has been a cost-effective investment for the government; coloured artisans, for instance, have contributed greatly to the building industry, at far lower wages than whites would have commanded.

However, oppression and conflict are not absent from coloured education. For instance, when a separate teachers training college for coloureds was opened in Windhoek (when a white college was also nearing completion) the walls were daubed with slogans. A local press report described the cleaning-up operation:

> Public works assisted as far as it could. A team of convicts were fetched from the Windhoek Central Prison and the Rector and Vice-Rector were issued with pistols. It was an unusual sight to see two learned men scrubbing and washing, with the butts of guns protruding from their pockets[16].

Attempts are also being made to draw coloured pupils into careers with the South African miliary through leadership courses.

University Education

As previously mentioned, Namibia does not have a University. This is not for financial reasons: the local white admininstration can afford to maintain 170 white teacher-trainees and 53 staff in a Windhoek College built at a cost of R18 million (£10m) and capable of taking 500 students[17].

Namibian students have therefore been directed to South African universities. According to official statistics (Table 10) there were 2 268 whites, 157 coloureds and 98 blacks from Namibia studying in South Africa in 1978.

---

16. *Windhoek Advertiser* 16 January 1978.
17. Education Branch, Administration for Whites, 1981 Report.

To these figures should be added the black Namibians enrolled with UNISA, the South African correspondence university. There were 63 such students in 1979[18].

Instead of a university, the South African government in 1980 started the Academy for Tertiary Education in Windhoek. The Academy is open to 'all races' but few whites have need of it. By 1982 the Academy was a substantial institution with a staff of 120 (comprising 62 lecturers and 58 administrative personnel) and about 500 full-time students (compare Table 9). Its budget for 1981/82 was R2.5 million[19].

The Academy has two branches. The largest one offers courses for those with a junior secondary certificate. This forms the 'College for Extended Education' and offers courses in commerce and school subjects (English, Afrikaans, Biology, Biblical Studies and Home Economics). The second section offers university courses (in association with the university of South Africa, a correspondence university) and some technical courses. This is the 'University and Technicon'. For these tertiary students staff are provided for tutoring in languages, Geography, Biblical Studies, South African and European History, Social Work, Zoology, Domestic Science, Education, Commerce, Engineering, and Medical Technology. The staff are almost all graduates of Afrikaans universities in South Africa[20].

The Academy plays an important role in South African educational strategy for Namibia. It offers opportunities for teachers (who can improve their salaries by studying) and for young Namibians who cannot be accommodated in the secondary schools, and who might otherwise leave the country in search of education in SWAPO and UN programmes. More black Namibians are being helped to take up jobs in government and commerce, so bolstering the small black middle class. In practice, however, tuition is not always of high quality, and the number of students who drop out before completing is thought to be significant.

The military are also taking a close interest in the Academy. The prospectus mentions that some studies will be helpful in a military career. For instance:

> History offers an excellent background for careers in the information service, National Intelligence, and the anthropological services of the armed forces and SWA Administration[21].

---

18. Melber 1979, p.192.
19. *Windhoek Advertiser*, 4 February 1982.
20. Academy for Tertiary Education 1983.
21. Ibid, p.20.

A further revelation of military and business collaboration in the Academy, perhaps flowing from frustration with the formal school structure, is made in the 1983 prospectus which announces a 'research project' in 'community development'. This project in fact has nothing to do with tertiary or secondary education, but is intended for illiterate adults. The intention is to reach 60 000 adults and to provide them with a specific trade and proficiency in languages, numeracy and 'socio-economics'. The first beneficiaries, however, will be members of the SWA Territorial Force[22].

This venture into adult education will apparently be South Africa's boldest attempt at obtaining the collaboration of black Namibians.

Proposals for Reform

In August 1983, the Advisory Committee for Human Sciences Research in SWA/Namibia published a report to the Department of National Education in Namibia. This report summarised the findings of a three-year research project, and urges a sophisticated restructuring of the education system. Its findings on the failure of the present education system in almost every area have been mentioned above. Taken together, they are devastating — perhaps one reason why the report has only been published in Afrikaans.

The detailed proposals of the Report are set out in Appendix 1 below. There are perhaps four principal thrusts:
- a new primary school syllabus stressing functional literacy and giving students 'modern values'.
- meeting the demand for skills within the economy by special vocational schools parallel with traditional academic secondary schools — at junior secondary level to produce 'operators' and at senior secondary level more skilled personnel.
- centralising control of education in view of the ineffectiveness of ethnic administrations.
- reinforcing the role of the private sector in education, especially through mining companies funding 'career training colleges' at senior secondary level.

There are two notable absences from the plan: a serious discussion of making education compulsory, and any commitment to English (functional literacy is to be either in English or Afrikaans, and the Report itself is of course in Afrikaans). The guiding light of the

---

22. Ibid, p.82.

South African Schooltexts for Namibia: RACE

South Africa is a multiracial society, the text says, but blacks are presented as anthropological curiosities.

Source: 'History, Standard 2': Jordaan & Jordaan (1983); 'History 4': Lambrechts, Van Schoor, Bester & Potgieter (1980); 'History, Standard 3': Jordaan & Jordaan (1983)

South Africa is a multiracial society.

WE HAVE LEARNT THE FOLLOWING
- The Wambos came into the country during the 16th and 17th centuries
- The Wambos live in the northern part of the country as well as in southern Angola
- There are eight Wambo tribes.
- The Wambos are dark people. They are not very tall.
- The men carried their knobkieries, pipes and snuff boxes under their aprons around their waists. The women were fond of ornaments.
- The men had more than one wife. Each man and each of his wives had their own huts, next to their lands. They formed a small village which was encircled by a high pole fence. At night the cattle slept inside the kraal.
- The sacred fire always burnt near the captain's hut.
- They were farmers. Their main food was a thick porridge made of mahangu wheat. They also ate fruit and vegetables and kept cattle and goats.
- The women tilled the soil, cooked the food and made the household utensils.
- The men herded the cattle, cleaned the waterholes and hunted for meat.
- They had bows made from the centre piece of a palm leaf. They also dipped their arrowheads in poison.
- They smelted iron and mined copper.
- The father gave a baby its name.
- Both the boys and girls had to go through an initiation ceremony before they could get married.
- The bridegroom had to supply an ox at his wedding feast. The wedding ceremony was a great feast.
- The captaincy was not inherited. All the ground belonged to the captain and the chiefs had to see that it was tilled.
- A captain's funeral varied from tribe to tribe.
- They had a strange form of punishment.
- The arrival of the Whites had a great influence on their way of life.

DO THE FOLLOWING
Complete the following main point scheme in your workbook by writing a short sentence or a few sentences next to each point.
1. The Wambos came from . . .
2. They lived in the area between . . . and . . .

Traditional Herero man.

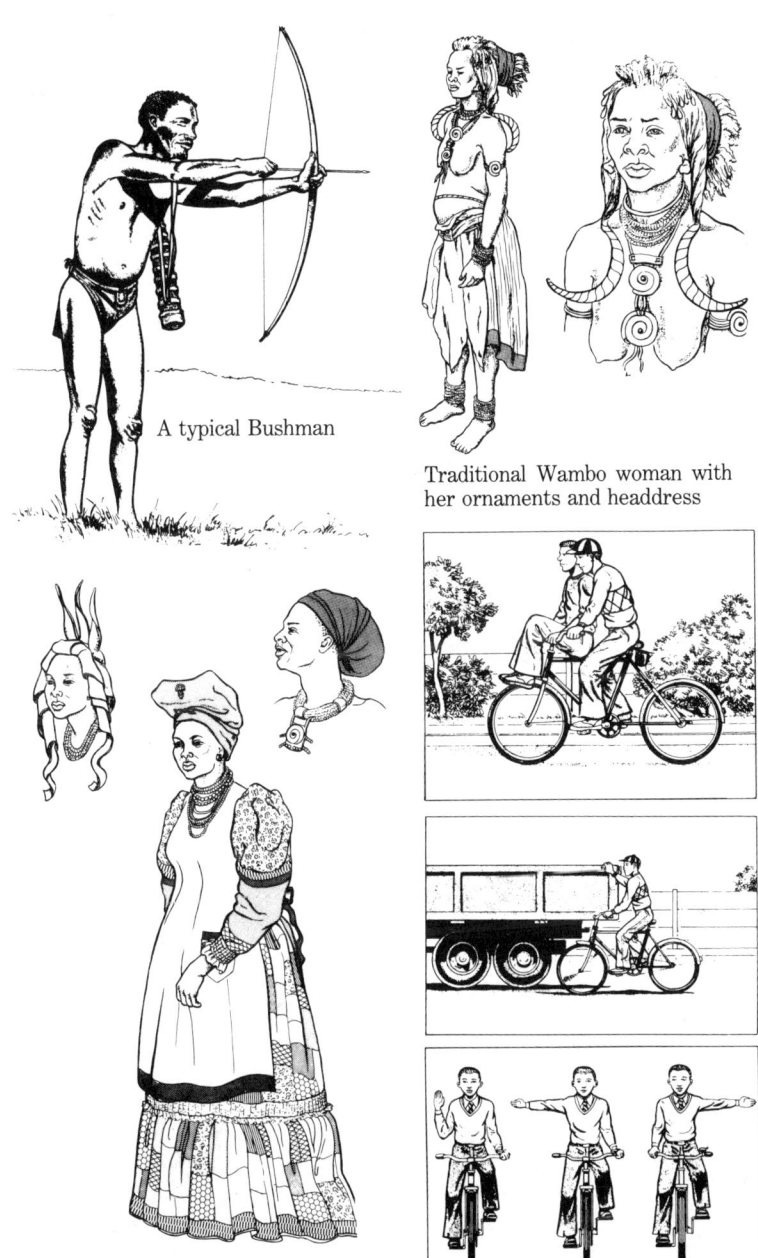

A typical Bushman

Traditional Wambo woman with her ornaments and headdress

A Herero woman and various headdresses

Report is the needs of the present economy, not education for all nor building national cohesion.

In fact the Report is based on the belief that Namibians need to be introduced to the values of a modern society, as symbolised by organisations like the great mining companies. It is asserted that the central problem of developing countries is that the 'traditional culture' of small farmers producing what they need for themselves can no longer be continued because there is now not enough land. People therefore enter a confused or 'transitional' culture between the traditional and the modern. Farming itself will have to change, with people owning their own land and no longer inheriting status. Others will have to move into industry. All this means that people need new values: for example, the Report argues that Namibians do not believe in the importance of hard work, and therefore need to be taught a 'work ethic'. The role of education is to enable people to make the changes necessary for participation in the complex technological and social institutions of modern culture[23].

In the same way, the Report thinks that pupils have to repeat years in school, not primarily because of the problems we have listed, but because they come to school out of a 'traditional culture' and an unstimulating home environment. They are not used to the values taught by school: they must therefore have a pre-primary school-readiness year, to change their views. Instead of building on pupils' experiences, they must be changed.

These assumptions do not stand up to examination. Firstly, in no sense can Namibians be seen as isolated farmers producing for their own subsistence, ignorant of the modern economy. Through a century of brutal colonisation, Namibians have been integrated into the modern economy as migrant workers; practically all families depend for at least some of their income on money coming back from a worker. Traditional family life changed completely as colonial rule was enforced, and workers had to leave their families behind. Namibians know all about the necessity for hard work, especially with wages as low as they have been this century. Can traditional values be all that strong in a country where 75% of the population is active in Christian churches? Is it not possible that the clash of values found in school has nothing to do with 'traditional' versus 'modern', but that Namibians on the basis of their own clear values reject the imposition of the values of apartheid?

Secondly, what is this 'modern society' to which Namibians are to be changed? The present economic structure is manifestly unjust, with very few jobs, gross inequalities in earnings, and ownership and

---

23.   ACHSR Vol. 5, 1983, pp.13f, 118f.

power reserved almost entirely for foreign companies and local whites. The 'modern values' of the present government, as experienced by ordinary Namibians especially in the war zones, include disrespect for human rights and the use of torture. The distinct coolness in the Report for the work of the churches, and the enthusiasm for large mining companies, does not augur well for the kind of 'modern attitudes' to be promoted[24].

Implementation of the Report would therefore be, at best, a mixed blessing: some elements, such as the emphasis on functional literacy, would be an improvement on the present situation; but the overall thrust of the recommendations is to keep non-white Namibians in subordinate positions. The state has still to respond officially to the Report, and some ethnic authorities are opposed to the erosion of their power and the lack of attention to English. Nevertheless, reform along these lines seems likely.

State Education by Other Methods

We have seen that large employers, in particular the mining companies, have their own training schemes. Government, as the largest employer of all, also has some. The state now runs a programme, through a college in Otjiwarongo, to train lower level African administrative staff. There is another for post office workers. Training is also being provided for some categories of railway workers, though this is restricted by the evident policy goal that Namibia's railways should be run indefinitely by South African Railways.

Radio has been second only to the schools in the consciousness-moulding operations of the South African government. Broadcasting services have been developed in several languages. Transmissions are almost all in the high frequency range (FM). This provides good (short-range) reception quality. But, more importantly, the government hopes to persuade people not to purchase short-wave radios with which they can listen to foreign broadcasts, especially those of SWAPO. The result is that the entire country can now be reached on FM. Standards of technical production are generally high. Slanted news broadcasts are interspersed with music and a variety of other cultural programmes. South African broadcasts are, even if not believed, generally listened to. The significance of radio in such a

---

24. Ibid, p.158, "(Private schools) which promote specific attitudes and value orientations which fit into the broad national framework should be financially supported".

sparsely populated country has not been lost on SWAPO, which now has six radio programmes beamed to Namibia from neighbouring African countries.

Television was introduced to Namibia in 1982. Little effort has been made to extend it into the rural African community. Rather, it is seen as a way of keeping South African officials happy. Almost all the programming is borrowed from South African Television.

The *libraries* to which Namibians have access are small, both in size and in number. The Windhoek public library, with a collection of about 60 000 books, remains closed to the black public. The same applies to six libraries in rural towns. Black schools do not have a state library service though the Department of National Education recently advertised for a person to start such a service. Three church secondary schools have quite good libraries. The Administration Library — an invaluable collection of books and articles about Namibia — was recently removed from the central government buildings and stored in the white teachers training college.

Education by Other Institutions

The inadequacy of the education provided by the state stimulates a demand for additional private or voluntary initiatives.

An early leader in this field was the Christian Centre, which has now become the *Council of Churches in Namibia*. Most of the major Namibian Churches (including Lutheran, Catholic, Anglican and Methodist, but not the pro-apartheid Dutch Reformed Church) are members of the Council. The most important educational programme of the Council is probably its organisation of study groups for adults who are learning English. At present there are 38 such groups with a total of about 600 pupils[25]. Hundreds of correspondence students are also organised into supportive groups and provided with some tutorial help. Community initiatives such as the Gibeon School and a few small co-operatives have been supported by the Council, which also provides bursaries for correspondence courses and study abroad. A variety of local and national meetings on topical issues are organised by the Council. The work of the Council is not allowed to continue unimpeded; two staff members working on education programmes were detained without charge in September 1983.

The Katatura Community Centre has taken over the migrant workers hostel, abandoned by the municipality, and provides facilities for local cultural groups and co-operatives. The Centre has

---

25. *CCN Information* (Newsletter) May 1983.

maintained its independence from the churches, municipality, and local businesses.

The first voluntary education programme in Namibia was the *Bureau of Literacy and Literature*, actually a branch of the same organisation in South Africa. The Bureau is now in the process of establishing itself as a Namibian organisation. Unfortunately, the Bureau has been plagued by organisational and political problems. However, in spite of a weak central organisation the Bureau had over 100 literacy groups in 1983, with an average of 15 learners per group[26]. This determination to learn, especially among women, indicates the great demand for adult education.

As we have seen, this is a demand which the *large companies* have recognised, both in providing adult education schemes for their employees and families, and in programmes for a wider community such as the literacy, needlework and now proposed agricultural training offered by the Rössing Foundation. The purpose of these programmes from the companies' point of view is to establish a favourable image by contributing to development, especially in the home areas of their migrant workforce. The companies do not see themselves as in conflict with the state's programme, but as supplementing it. Their attitude may be contrasted with the decision by Martin Luther High School and Gibeon School not simply to build an extra secondary school, but to adopt a syllabus from outside South Africa.

Searching for a Better Understanding of the World

At the start of this chapter, education was defined not simply as learning, but as searching for a better understanding of the world. Radio and television are part of the South African attempt to communicate its view of the world. There are, however, other channels and other views discussed in Namibia.

Elsewhere, *the press* would be one forum, but in Namibia it is not a strong institution. Because of the smallness of the literate population, newspapers are thin and do not have a large market. Papers which criticise the government do so at their peril. The Lutheran press at Oniipa has been blown up on two occasions within the past decade, and recently survived a South African shell passing through its roof. The *Windhoek Observer* (circulation of about 10 000), an independent English language weekly, plays an important and courageous role in Namibia, publishing reports of atrocities and

---

26. Brauer 1983.

corruption of the kind which would seldom appear in South Africa. Half a dozen other papers are published in various languages by political parties and the Churches. A recent development has been a series of meetings in Windhoek under the title *The Education Forum*, which has provided a platform for educated Namibians to exchange views on political affairs.

With two out of three Namibians counting themselves as Christians, *the Churches* are the most important institutions for nonformal education. Through regular worship services, catechetical and confirmation groups, Sunday schools, newspapers and other informative publications, choirs, youth groups, women's organisations, pastoral work, travel and cross-cultural contacts, the churches constitute a pervasive network for communication about vital issues. The Churches have been in the forefront of attempts to achieve education in spite of Bantu Education. Many schools, for instance, use church buildings because of the lack of classrooms, and most priests and ministers have a role in the local school. The Council of Churches has an important co-ordinating function, in addition to the specific educational programmes discussed earlier.

The church has provided space for the development of self-expression, discussion, democratic leadership and reflection. This process has made the churches more and more critical of the South African government. In particular, the South African authorities have been angered by widely disseminated open letters to South African Prime Ministers and pastoral letters to congregations which have bluntly condemned South African policies, especially the use of torture. In response, the South African forces have tried to muzzle the churches — a largely counter-productive attempt. Church life is being transformed by this political challenge. Many Namibians are finding a new relevance in their Bibles, practically the only literature widely available in the Namibian languages. Many groups are composing new hymns and prayers to give expression to their hope for liberation. And many Christians are joining in the struggle for liberation where practical opportunities present themselves.

Indeed, *political organisations* provide much significant education. The emergence of a national liberation movement is in itself a profoundly educational experience, challenging the humiliated to change their circumstances through their own joint efforts. For instance, we have this report on how Herman ya Toivo, one of the founding fathers of SWAPO, set about the task of organising Namibians in the 1950s:

> At that time I had no idea what meetings were for and how they could get people to communicate with each other and discuss their problems. Two

things were done in those meetings: first each one talked about his own problems and needs, and then they discussed the needs of any fellow Namibians who were in trouble or who needed help. This was followed by a general discussion to decide how much money each person at the meeting should give to help those in distress . . .[27]

The extent to which this actually happens is difficult to assess, but the SWAPO political programme of 1976 certainly instructs its organisers to adopt an eminently educational style in their work. They should:
— live in ordinary Namibian communities
— find out what problems people have in their daily lives, and
— enter into dialogue with oppressed groups about what can be done about these problems.

Several other political and cultural organisations have, of course, also contributed to the development of political consciousness in Namibia, and especially an awareness of colonial oppression. However, it is important to realise that inside Namibia the constraints of routine police repression and widespread illiteracy mean that people who have had the opportunity to read and to study in depth concepts such as capitalism or socialism would be the rare exceptions rather than the rule.

Education in exile also faces constraints — including the background of illiteracy and a lack of resources. But it has also provided the opportunity for experiment, and to that we now turn.

---

27. Winter 1976, p.186f.

3 Education through Exile

A total of some 70 000 Namibians are now in exile. Only a minority are involved in the armed struggle. The majority find themselves in refugee communities in Angola and Zambia where education is part of the daily struggle for survival and development. The refugees' education is, mostly, organised by SWAPO and the movement has therefore accumulated important experience. This experience will influence the way in which education is run in an independent Namibia.

History

One of the earliest aspirations of Namibian leaders — predating the establishment of any political party — was to send young Namibians abroad for education so that they could take a lead in the opposition to South African rule. The first exiles, who managed to escape Namibia in the late 1950s and early 1960s, accordingly started as many scholarship programmes as they could. Throughout the 1960s Namibians continued to flee their homeland. However, with Angola still under Portuguese rule, the annual number of refugees was probably counted in hundreds rather than thousands. Most of them made their way to Zambia.

In 1966 SWAPO launched its first attack on a South African police station. The South African forces reacted with campaigns of mass arrests and the torture of suspects. Herman ya Toivo, one of SWAPO's founding fathers, was sentenced to life imprisonment. The number of refugees began to increase.

A new wave of protest came in 1971, when the World Court in The Hague handed down its opinion that South Africa should withdraw its administration from Namibia. Secondary school pupils throughout the country demonstrated their support. And, breaking a long silence, the Churches welcomed the World Court opinion because of South African disregard for fundamental human rights.

All this came to head in the general strike by migrant workers at the end of 1971. A teacher, Johannes Nangutuuala, was chosen as the spokesman of the strikers. The strike was broken through the introduction of emergency regulations, prohibiting meetings and giving the police virtually unlimited powers of arrest, which persuaded more Namibians to flee.

By 1973 there were enough Namibians in Zambia for SWAPO to open a school for several hundred children on a farm outside Lusaka. In 1974 a SWAPO syllabus was devised for these schools, drawing mainly on the Zambian curriculum, with some borrowing from Tanzania too[1].

Tension continued to mount inside Namibia. In 1973 SWAPO successfully organised a complete boycott of the Ovamboland bantustan elections. This was followed by the flogging of suspected SWAPO supporters. In 1974 the Portuguese dictatorship fell, bringing independence for Angola, and a very rapid escalation of military activity by SWAPO and South Africa. Namibians began crossing into Angola (and from there to Zambia) in their thousands, in what became known as the 'Exodus'.

The largest number of the refugees were young people intent not only on fighting for independence but on gaining an education. There was a high proportion of women as it was they who were forced to bear the brunt of South African round-ups, interrogation, and arbitrary shooting. At this time too, South African officials in northern Namibia inspired the public flogging of suspected SWAPO supporters, whether men or women. Ill-trained and ill-disciplined tribal police were set up. Nurses, teachers, secondary school pupils, and educated persons were prime suspects.

SWAPO, therefore, had to create a system for coping first with a flood, and then a steady stream, of refugees. It was decided that the camps would be run by SWAPO rather than any relief organisation, because of the inevitable political dependence which would be associated with such organisations.

Not all the children could be transported to Zambia and a school was therefore started at Kassinga in southern Angola. However, in May 1978 (on Ascension Day) the school was raided by South African paratroopers who indiscriminately killed 600 of the refugees. A new Namibian 'health and education centre' was established further north, in the Kwanza Sul Province of Angola[2].

---

1. Mbamba 1979, p.7.
2. Ibid, p.23.

Material from SWAPO Women's Council Experimental Literacy Campaign: HOUSING

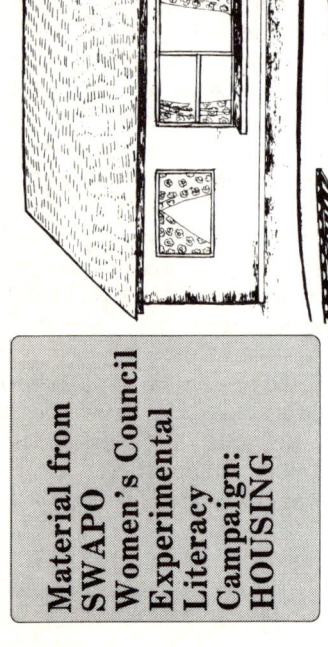

Discussion questions for literacy group:
1. What do you see in this picture?
2. Who lives in each kind of house?
Share ideas in the whole group.
3. Why do some people live in the compounds?
Do they like it? Why or why not?
Who decides they should live there?
4. Where would they like to live?
5. Why do only white people live in the big houses?
6. How do people become rich?
7. Is it fair that some people have very big houses and others are crowded in very small houses?
8. What changes in housing will we need to make in Namibia after Independence?
Share ideas in the whole group on this last question.
Summarise the main ideas the group made about housing in Namibia after Independence.

Source: *Literacy Leaders' Handbook, Feb 1983*

The Structure of Formal Education

Today the Kwanza Sul school has 8 000 — 10 000 pupils depending on the flow of arrivals and departures. The school in Zambia has 2 000 — 2 500 pupils[3]. Construction programmes for classrooms and dormitories are in progress at both places. In general, however, the facilities are very limited. SWAPO also has perhaps a total of a thousand pupils at its own secondary and primary schools on the Isle of Youth in Cuba. These schools are administered by SWAPO, but together with neighbouring Cuban and other nationalities' schools, participate in agricultural work as part of the curriculum.

The structure provides for kindergartens (which are essential as mothers have other work to do, and are occasionally away for study abroad), followed by six years of primary education and three years of secondary education. In Angola a 'pre-school' section has been instituted where remedial courses are offered in various Namibian languages so that children and young adults are better able to cope with English instruction in the main school. Learning English is the major task of the first three stages of school. The other main subjects are writing, mathematics, social studies, environmental and health studies, and 'creative activities' (arts, games, gardening, etc.). Each 'stage' is roughly equivalent to a normal school year, but often takes longer to cover in the refugee settlements[4].

Recently the teachers have been organised into seminar groups for each subject. The groups meet each Saturday to plan the next week's lessons. Lesson plans and materials are therefore being developed in a down-to-earth way, and in a few years should produce the basis for the publication of text books, provided that sufficiently detailed teachers' records are available. Namibian history/geography texts are being developed in a programme of cooperation between Bremen University and the UN Institute for Namibia.

Initially it was SWAPO policy to appoint to the Angolan and Zambian schools teachers who had completed some study abroad, for instance in West African secondary schools, and who were awaiting their next placement. This was not a success, because of their lack of teacher-training and the rapid turnover as teachers moved on to new jobs. Teacher-training programmes are now in operation to provide a more professional and permanent corps of teachers. However, a serious shortage of teachers persists and class sizes are probably about the same as in Namibia (minimum of 40 per class).

---

3. Figures in this chapter from interviews with SWAPO education officials.
4. Each stage can therefore accommodate pupils of different ages. Mbamba 1979, p.11f; Department of Education and Culture 1983.

Further Education Abroad

Since the first Namibian refugees fled, exiles with sufficient qualifications, obtained either inside or outside Namibia, have moved on to further education round the world. In all, about 5 000 Namibians have studied abroad through the efforts of many governments, ranging from the GDR to the United Kingdom, and international organisations, such as the United Nations, the Commonwealth Secretariat, the EEC, the Lutheran World Federation, and the World University Service. In spite of their desire for schooling, even those Namibians who have completed secondary education in Namibia have received such a poor grounding that many need courses in basic English and Mathematics before they can cope with university or even secondary education. Remedial courses specifically intended for Namibians are now being developed.

As Namibia is a UN mandated country, the United Nations has taken a close interest in education of refugees. The most important single institution has been the United Nations Institute for Namibia (UNIN) based in Lusaka. The Institute opened in 1976, and has trained some 500 Namibians. Most have been trained in administration, and would be able to move into civil service posts in an independence government. There will indeed be a real need for middle-level administrators, as some 20% of government posts are already estimated to be vacant, and it is anticipated that many whites in the present administration will leave at the time of independence, because of their total antipathy to a SWAPO government. UNIN students can specialise in education, agriculture, or administration, on top of a grounding in economics and development theory. Before graduating, trainees spend at least six months on a placement with one or other friendly Third World government. UNIN now also trains secretaries and teachers.

Under the umbrella of the United Nations Nationhood Programme for Namibia several groups of Namibians have since 1978 been prepared for special tasks. There have been, for instance, courses for magistrates, postal workers, radio technicians, pilots, aircraft engineers, and nutritionists. Sectoral studies of the Namibian economy are in progress.

Other Education in the Camps

Adult education programmes are provided on a self-help basis, particularly by the SWAPO Women's Council. The motivation to take part in adult education is strong, with an emphasis on learning

English and acquiring other basic school qualifications. These are of course a pre-requisite for further studies abroad.

There is a shortage of materials suitable for adults. However, a programme to train literacy teachers and produce discussion materials has recently been launched. The Namibia Extension Unit is a new SWAPO venture based in Zambia and utilising correspondence methods and study groups to reach the settlements. Materials for English and Mathematics have been produced, and tutorial groups involving about 2 000 adults have recently been established in some settlements. In the longer term it is intended that the Extension Unit should engage in vocational training.

A number of self-help projects have been established in the settlements, including agricultural projects, several tailoring workshops, a weaving project, a typing school, a poultry farm and a shoemaking unit. Projects are also underway to train builders who can produce building materials from local resources. This will alleviate the great accommodation shortage in the settlements, which still depend on tents for shelter. Namibians from the settlements are also being trained in water technologies such as drilling wells, and setting up pumps.

A UN vocational training centre for 200 Namibians has been built in Kwanza Sul Province of Angola in cooperation with the International Labour Organisation (ILO). Carpentry, building, electrical work, plumbing, and other trades will be taught when the centre opens during 1983/84. A secondary school specialising in technical training is planned for the Congo. A trade union school is run in the settlements by the Finnish trade unions.

Finally, Namibians have opportunities for informal education through movements such as the young pioneers, the Youth League, the Womens' Council, the Elders' Council, and sports teams. Religious education continues through the ecumenical chaplaincy, a part of SWAPO, in which several pastors and priests serve.

An impressive educational programme has therefore been built up from nothing over the past ten years. However, these efforts are still interrupted and limited by the reality and the threat of South African raids and destabilisation of Angola and Zambia. The numbers educated are still well short of requirements for specific tasks. The poverty of education in Namibia means that there is always a shortage of skilled people to lead and manage new programmes.

Present Considerations

The maintenance of education in the settlements depends on international solidarity, and this dependence is uncomfortable. While this solidarity is meeting real and basic needs — and indirectly helps to educate people in many countries about southern Africa — it is clearly not desirable that Namibians should depend on international aid in the long term. A major area to which SWAPO is now giving higher priority is food production, to improve self-reliance. SWAPO is also considering organising agricultural production in the settlements so that it is part of the curriculum for secondary school pupils. This may be influenced by the ideas of Cuban schools which are linked to the countryside and take part in agricultural production.

As it becomes more likely that Namibian independence is several years away, more attention is being given to mass education programmes, such as distance teaching and adult literacy. More programmes of this nature, managed by Namibians, may be needed in future, given the educational needs of existing refugees and the possibility of another flood of exiles at any time. Such mass education programmes may also be of direct use after independence.

An important area for SWAPO is political education[5]. Political ideas, except of the most basic kind, are not easily shaped by didactic propaganda. The political educator must also be a skilled listener, able to facilitate discussion so that people gain the confidence to analyse their own circumstances and decide upon programmes of joint action. Experience of decision-making and management of social programmes is also important. However, the high degree of discipline which is apparently necessitated by the security situation means that there are not many areas in which decision-making can be 'decentralised'. Clearly the refugees have been through harrowing experiences, and have definite ideas about the need to end South African rule in Namibia. They may also require the tools to study the structures of their country, and the role they themselves might be able to play in reconstruction when they return.

Policy

The experience of education in exile has informed reflection and discussion on future education policy for an independent Namibia. It is important to examine SWAPO policy: observers ranging from the South African army to the churches are agreed that SWAPO is the most likely party to form an independence government after free elections. SWAPO is radically opposed to South African education policy, as is evident from a recent SWAPO paper:

Bantu Education is a political weapon in the hands of the ruling white

---

5. Mbamba 1979, p.39f; Mbamba 1982, p.135f.

oligarchy against the dispossessed African majority. Bantu Education is a travesty of all precepts of education as understood by the large majority of mankind. It sought to build reinforced tribal cocoons in which antiquarian sentiments are glorified. A new education system for free Namibia must therefore be an antithesis of the present system of education in the country[6].

The appreciation that there must be a link-up between political change and a new kind of education in Namibia is also reflected in a recent statement by SWAPO President, Sam Nujoma:

> It is through education, formal and informal, that we gain understanding of the various forces which act against or in support of the people's quest for freedom and independence . . . Culture defines our authenticity, our personality and our role as creators of a new socio-political order in Namibia . . . Revolution only has historical meaning when translated into the way of living of a people. In a revolutionary situation, Education and Culture interact in a dynamic way in the moulding and creation of a new man: a liberated man. Basic education is a must for every young Namibian. Adult education and vocational training are rights which must be seized upon by every adult[7].

At a seminar on education in Lusaka during September 1982 SWAPO narrowed down its present priorities to three areas: teacher training; curriculum development; and research into the present and future education system[8].

The striving for education is therefore a high priority for the exiled Namibians. It is an integral part of the struggle for independence and human development. The leaders of SWAPO are totally opposed to the kind of education experienced in Namibia, and, in spite of immense difficulties, are now starting to build a new system of education. This is proving to be a slow process, partly because of the exigencies of war, partly because of a shortage of skilled Namibian educators, and partly because new concepts of education must be discussed with large numbers of people before they can be implemented. But it is underway.

---

6. Angula 1982 c, p.1.
7. Message to Seminar on Education and Culture for Liberation in Southern Africa, 1981.
8. Angula 1982 c, p.22.

4 Come Independence

The Context of Independence

When independence does come to Namibia, education will be a national preoccupation. The starting point for any discussion on educational policy after independence must be the policies of the likely government. We therefore deal extensively below with the present views of SWAPO. However, changes in Namibia's education system will inevitably be accompanied by the emergence of conflicts and contradictions. The government will find itself exposed to pressures from groups such as parents and teachers, whose expectations have been moulded under present colonial society.

The independence government will face other constraints whose extent will depend on the circumstances of the time and the terms of the independence settlement. If independence comes in the 1980s, resources of all kinds — skilled personnel, finance and buildings — are likely to be severely limited, especially if the economy has continued its present decline intensified by the destruction caused by war.

With these constraints in mind, the broad outlines of the educational challenges which the independence government will face are already clear:
- Establishing a wide variety of technical and professional training programmes. An authoritative estimate of the skilled manpower needs in Namibia after independence, taking account of the probable recruitment of expatriate 'replacements', shows that the need will be extensive (Table 11).
- Establishing for a large majority of the population (both adults and children) the basic education programmes denied them at present.
- Advancing national cohesion, in the face of ethnic prejudices and structures which reflect a century of colonial rule. The promotion

of English as a national language is seen as a major part of this nation-building. It will be a major task, as English is at present not spoken widely.
- Tackling the problems caused by the recent South African promotion of a relatively well-paid middle-class, including teachers. These inequalities have to be reduced if resources are to be made available for development programmes benefiting the people as a whole. But at the same time it could be an area of considerable conflict with some teachers.
- Establishing programmes of a social and political nature to help Namibians overcome the colonial legacy and participate in the creation of a new society. The effects of a century of repression and exploitation are all too evident, including a lack of family life, disease which could be avoided, and alcoholism. A dramatic reduction in migrant labour and the release of resources for new agricultural and industrial projects will improve conditions; new health services will be established; but skilled community workers will also be needed to work on a very local level (where central government cannot reach) and enable people to meet some of their basic needs through their joint efforts. Similarly, the UNIN study on Agrarian Reform in Namibia recommends that there should be large-scale rural adult education programmes and that such education should not be restricted to a technical agricultural extension service, but should raise political awareness and assist rural people to organise themselves and influence government policy[1].
- In spite of the scale of all these needs, educational programmes must be devised and implemented without bankrupting the treasury and within the available numbers of skilled personnel.

SWAPO Policy

The probable general objectives of a SWAPO government's educational policy to meet these challenges have been laid out in several documents[2].
They include:
1. Nine years of compulsory basic education for every child 7-16 years old.
2. Emphasis during the last three years of basic education and

---
1. UNIN (Mshonga) 1979, p.71.
2. See Angula, Mbamba, Tjitendero and SWAPO in bibliography.

secondary education on agriculture, technology and vocational training.
3. Introduction of English as a national language through adult and basic education.
4. Spreading political and moral awareness, explaining the policies of the new government, promoting participation in local and national unity, and eliminating ethnic prejudices.
5. Establishment of creches, day-care centres and kindergartens.
6. Elimination of all discriminatory and apartheid structures in education so that provision for all citizens is free and equal.
7. Widespread adult and nonformal education programmes, especially at work-places.

Expansion of Schooling

Such plans require an expansion of schooling. SWAPO's own hope is that in five years of independence, the proportion of children completing six years' primary education can be raised from the present level of about 40% to 75%; and half of those would then go on to lower secondary school (compared with about 35% at present). By the twentieth year of independence, all children would have a full nine years' compulsory basic education[3].

There will be great popular demand for more schooling. The experience of Angola, Mozambique and Zimbabwe was that within two years of independence the school population had doubled. No matter what growth rate the government may plan for increasing enrolments, parents are going to take the initiative: they are going to set up schools where there were none, and where schools already exist they will add on classrooms. Additional teachers will be 'appointed' in one way or another to cope with the massive new intake of pupils. Through the local party branch, the government will come under effective pressure to recognise the steps taken. The government will anyway want to comply, as it will not want to suppress popular initiative.

There will be a heavy demand for more teachers, at a time when the ablest are leaving for new jobs in government and commerce. An enormous teacher-training capacity will be needed. The number of teachers who will need training could be perhaps 5 000 (ten times the present capacity). One possible way to make some impression on this need would be to take over about six of the high schools and hostels presently reserved for whites and convert them into teacher-training

---

3. Angula 1982 c, p.21f.

institutions. If, after some time, there is an excessive teacher-training capacity, some of the colleges could revert to secondary schools.

There will still be a tremendous shortage of qualified teachers. This is unavoidable, as the school population will probably be in the region of half a million (double the present enrolment) two years after independence. The only obvious way of dealing with this explosion would be to employ senior primary school pupils and secondary school pupils, on a part-time basis and for a nominal fee, as assistant teachers. This tuition would also help the older pupils to clarify what they have learnt in the lower grades. Experience elsewhere suggests, however, that this is feasible only if it is accompanied by real in-service training and support; otherwise, the risk is that the teaching will be confused and of poor quality.

Finance is likely to be in almost as short supply as teachers. It will be essential, if spending on schooling is not to get out of hand, to re-examine the present level of teachers' salaries; this is considered futher below. Money can also be saved on school building programmes. Instead of large contractors and expensive materials, perfectly adequate classrooms and teachers' houses can be built with local materials and improved traditional building methods. The participation of local people could mean local employment at a moderate cost.

A New Curriculum

The risk is that this pressure for more schools will overwhelm the government's other priorities, such as changing the content of education. Building schools is relatively straight-forward. It is also likely to be more immediately popular than some aspects of a new syllabus. Parents' expectations are inevitably moulded by what they have experienced, and their demand, initially, may well be for more of the kind of schools they know about. Some, denied for so long the kind of education offered to whites, may even see that as a model — as a route to a secure job. Conversely, some may criticise the teaching of agricultural skills as being a return to 'Bantu Education'. Other innovations, however, especially the emphasis on English, will command widespread enthusiasm.

At a seminar in September 1982 SWAPO produced an outline of a new curriculum[4]:

(a) *Pre-school:* social development and play activities introducing children to learning skills.

---

4. Angula 1982 c, p.11f.

(b) *Lower Primary (first three years of basic education):* Basic skills of reading, writing and communication in the mother tongue; social development; basic communication skills in English; mathematics; personal and community hygiene; arts and sports; gardening and other productive school activities. The mother tongue will be the medium of instruction.

(c) *Upper Primary (second three years of basic education):* English will gradually take over as the medium of instruction. Subjects to include: English, mother tongue, mathematics, environmental studies, social sciences, arts and sports. There will also be gardening and other manual activities to encourage a positive attitude towards work.

(d) *Lower Secondary (last three years of basic education):* An *academic* component including communication skills in English, mathematics, biology, physics, chemistry and development studies (integrating history, geography and economics). A *cultural* component including literature in English and mother tongue, foreign language, music and dance, moral and political education, physical and health education, sports, clubs, and youth organisations. A *skills development* component with options for carpentry, plumbing, mechanics, electrician's training, printing, textiles, commercial and design studies. Agriculture would be compulsory.

(e) Three alternative forms of further secondary education: *upper secondary*, which would be an amplification of the lower secondary curriculum; *vocational training*, which would be training in specific occupations and (presumably) shorter in duration than upper secondary education; and *technical training* in skills such as carpentry.

(f) At a higher level, students may be selected for advanced technical and professional training or for university studies. It can be assumed that an independent Namibia would quickly establish a university. However, with only perhaps a thousand students with standard university entrance qualifications, the Namibian university may not confine itself to degree-level courses. It may be closely linked with technical and research institutes.

SWAPO's plans for introducing a system of free and compulsory basic education — including an emphasis on preparation for work — is in line with most development thinking about education. It is important that such basic education programmes be complete and useful in themselves: of value to those who leave after basic education, and not just for those going on to further and higher levels of education[5].

Teaching methods will be as important as the content of basic

---

5. See Coombs 1973, p.14f for a list of skills which can be included in basic education.

education. One expert on basic education stresses methods of teaching which 'rouse curiosity, develop self-reliance, and encourage physical and mental adaptability'[6]. This means intensive teacher training and retraining, as SWAPO already recognises.

Inevitably, the introduction of English is going to be difficult, but most educationalists would probably concur with the approach which SWAPO apparently envisages: reading and writing in the mother tongue, simultaneously starting with *verbal* English, and then reading and writing in English. These and other issues are examined in detail in a UNIN study on language policy.[7]

The Relationship Between Education and Work

The relationship between education and work is a crucial one, and it is an area still under discussion within SWAPO. It is proposed to include preparations for work within the final three-year cycle of basic education. This will mean providing for an annual intake of about 40 000 pupils per year, roughly eight times the current provision. The inputs of trained staff, equipment, materials and land are potentially very expensive — considerably more than for the first two cycles of basic education. Under these circumstances, a possible direction would be:
1. Concentrating on food-production skills: crops, vegetable growing, livestock raising etc.
2. Additional experience in skills which are likely to be useful in more than one field of technology: practical use of mathematics for measurement and calculation, use of hand tools for basic wood and metal work, use of electricity and motors, etc. An accurate list of such fundamental skills should be worked out with those who might provide further training or employment.
3. As important as a specific productive skill is *the ability to analyse a productive process*. In some Zimbabwean schools, pupils undertake projects to investigate local industry or establish their own agricultural or other enterprise. The aim is to understand the process of identifying resources, production, distribution, and monitoring so that improvements can be made[8].

Very bold innovation is needed in Namibia in the field of technical/professional work training after basic education. Basic education is intended to provide a nine-year education which is both

---

6. Phillips 1975, p.126.
7. UNIN 1979.
8. Robson 1982.

complete in itself, and relevant to the needs of all citizens. Experience elsewhere in the world suggests, however, that employers unwittingly apply constant pressure to increase the number of years of education without making it any more relevant. Where school certificates are used to select people for better-paying jobs, there is a tendency for certificates to become an end in themselves. This problem cannot be cured simply by changing education policy. Nevertheless, whilst senior secondary schools will clearly be needed, it may perhaps help if most technical post-basic education was provided for people already in employment, or for whom specific vacancies exist.

There are other reasons for making this change. Full-time technical education is very often not only inefficient, but also very expensive. The high cost of the various UN-sponsored Vocational Training Programmes for Namibians in exile can perhaps be justified in view of the extreme needs of Namibians at present. If independence is to be real, however, Namibians must find cheaper ways of providing much more technical education.

One possible approach is to concentrate on part-time, in-service, work-related courses for people already in employment. For the individual this would mean some or all of the following:

- attendance each year at several short, full-time courses (of less than a month);
- night classes;
- weekend study sessions each month;
- half days off each week for study;
- correspondence courses;
- study groups with a tutor at the place of work.

For the government it would mean setting up institutes to provide post-basic technical training in, for instance, agriculture, mining, public administration, teaching, building trades, health, fishing, cooperatives, etc. Facilities for study should be provided at or near workplaces, where possible. The advantage of such education is that pupils learn more about what they are already doing, and so are more able to grasp new skills. For instance, no formal school course is offered for nurses in Namibia (or in many other countries). Yet many Namibians have been efficiently trained for this profession, studying part-time or in-between their duties. It is important, at the same time, that post-basic education should not focus too narrowly on technical skills, in order to avoid the danger of a technocratic elite. Basic education should have provided adequate study skills for people to study additional subjects, by correspondence.

'In-employment' education may not be able to provide all the skill-training which is needed. However, it will be worthwhile to examine the justification for any long term, full-time training with some strictness.

It is also in this area of post-basic and pre-university education that room may be found for projects in 'education with production', as another form of work-related/in-service education. This philosophy of eduction stresses that schools should produce as well as consume. This will give pupils an understanding of the reality of work; they will see the usefulness of what they are learning, and any profits from what they produce can defray the costs of their education. Experience in Zimbabwe, however, has shown that it is not easy to introduce education with production, in spite of its attractions. There are also many examples elsewhere of education with production having increased costs rather than contributed profits. The areas of difficulty appear to be the following:

- The staff are qualified as teachers, and naturally tend to devote most of their effort to teaching academic subjects and technical skills, rather than running a profitable enterprise.
- The students are not credited in the examination system for their practical skill and sheer hard labour; the time spent in work, in fact, puts them at a disadvantage compared to full-time students who spend most of their time with their books.
- Students provide (part-time) labour, but other inputs such as land, seeds, tools, machines and building materials are also needed. Hired labourers may also be needed to cover school holidays or other breaks. All these are expensive, and often not easily available from the education department.
- Academic subjects such as mathematics and science ought to be integrated and relevant to the production in which the students and teachers are engaged; but skilled (and additional) staff are needed to adapt the syllabus in this way.

This does not mean that education with production should be discarded. On the contrary, there have been successes, such as in training builders in Zimbabwe. It can be a significant means of employment generation, if the various departments of government are willing and able to provide *all* the inputs and support which are necessary for success in a new venture.

The relationship between education and work has inevitably to be linked to the consideration of how much people are paid for different jobs. There can be little doubt, for example, that given the level of teachers' salaries compared to what a small farmer can earn, the students of Namibia are today acting rationally in seeking every chance to become teachers rather than improve their agricultural expertise. This issue of income distribution is delicate and difficult — but any serious education policy will have to take it into account.

Mass Adult Education Programmes

With 60% of the population illiterate and only a small fraction understanding English, education cannot be confined to children. Literacy is essential for the building of political awareness as well as for technical education and public health campaigns. SWAPO plans to halve adult illiteracy in ten years, and to ensure that all Namibians are literate after twenty years of independence. Considerable experience is being generated in exile. Women especially are taking a lead, both inside and outside the country. The position of women is a key target for change in independent Namibia. This will mean attention to the educational and organisational needs of women, and also adjustments in the situation of men and the family. Such programmes in adult education require parallel development of the press and broadcasting. They also require money: adult education has proved elsewhere to be more cost-effective than schooling, but it is still not cheap.

One of the most interesting models for adult education is that generated by the Brazilian educator Paulo Freire, and those who work with grass-roots Christian communities in Latin America. Freire attacks the idea that education has to do with the acquisition of knowledge, as a fixed and tradeable commodity. Rather, education must be seen as a process, a dialogue in which people learn from one another and reflect on their actions, so that they gain confidence and learn to 'read' their reality and 'write' their own history. Education thus gives people the power to decide and act for their collective interests.

A literacy campaign on this kind of model in Namibia would be a major and prolonged effort. Following the dictum that 'an illiterate person is outside politics', it is socialist states which, despite enormous difficulties, have made the most rapid progress towards universal literacy. However, dramatic campaigns to abolish illiteracy, as in Nicaragua and Cuba, are not *yet* possible in Namibia. Cuba started with 70% literacy and a common language with an established literature. They could spare more skilled people for longer than will be the case in post-independence Namibia.

Any Namibian literacy campaign would therefore have to build up its momentum steadily, until such time as it has the resources to undertake an acceleration. Once a literacy census has been conducted, services would have to be built up in journalism, writing, printing and broadcasting. Linguistic analysis would have to be completed, and follow-up courses in English and various vocations for adults must be available, so that people do not become literate only to discover that their new skill is not very useful. A variety of institutions must be

Material from SWAPO Women's Council Experimental Literacy Campaign: GROUP DISCUSSION

Discussion questions for literacy groups:
1. What is happening in this picture?
2. Why are communal meetings necessary?
3. How can they be used to build unity and co-operation?
Ask the people to make small groups to discuss:

4. Think of different meetings you have attended both inside and outside the camp. What things make a meeting good? What things make a meeting frustrating? *Share* in the whole group. Then ask,
5. Why is it important that everyone should have a chance to speak, knowing that they will be listened to?
6. What can we do to encourage people to speak and to listen to each other carefully at meetings?
Summarise the points the group has made. If they decide on an action, help them.

Source: *Literacy Leaders' Handbook Feb 1983*

motivated to take part in literacy work. Women's organisations and the churches should be especially drawn into the programme: the work-place literacy programmes envisaged by SWAPO would not reach all sectors of the population.

Soon after independence the foundations for a campaign could be laid by a few teams of educators and researchers, each team working in a carefully selected small area, to develop methods and materials for basic adult education. The team would need a base in the community, which could also be a meeting place and resource centre for the local people. The main learners in this phase would be the team, as they discover the issues that concern people, and as they join with local groups in trying to find a way of tackling the problems they confront in their daily lives. Once good methods have been developed they could be spread, relying especially on structures such as those of the churches, farmers' groups, workplace organisations, youth groups, women's organisations, etc. An important source of staff for literacy work might be demobilised combatants from the guerrilla army.

If the literacy campaign is to be genuinely two-way, allowing participants as well as leaders to express themselves, it will be essential to provide thorough training for adult educators. If 100 000 Namibians are to be involved as learners in the literacy campaign some years hence, at least 4 000 part-time group leaders and perhaps 200 full-time professional adult educators must be trained, and an institute with at least 30 staff persons established to provide back-up services. The cost including materials, transport, etc, would be in the region of R10 million per year (about R100 per adult learner) at present-day Namibian prices.

The Role of the Churches

Discussion so far has concentrated on the role of the state. Because of political oppression, Namibia has relatively few independent and voluntary bodies. The exceptions are the churches, which, with 70% of the population Christian, provide an unequalled network for communication and social organisation in Namibia, especially in the rural areas.

The controversy surrounding church criticism of South African occupation of Namibia has created a basic political awareness in the churches. Relations between SWAPO and the Namibian churches are likely to remain co-operative, but the churches will certainly insist on maintaining their autonomous role as religious bodies with the right to criticise any abuse of power. Of course, it is also true that the churches themselves are in need of criticism, for instance, in the limited role allowed to women, and persistent ethnic division. It is also necessary to take account of the churches' lack of familiarity with development projects led by local groups.

There is a great opportunity for bodies such as the Council of Churches in Namibia to undertake more programmes to support groups tackling common problems in education, health and agriculture. A first step in this direction might be the formation throughout the country of inter-denominational groups who can analyse their community and the effects of their attempts to change it.

At present, church facilities are often used during the week as extra classroom space. No doubt this practice will continue. A question for both church and state is the future role of the private secondary schools presently run by the churches. These schools are highly regarded by Namibians, but the churches find it impossible to pay the salaries offered in the state sectors.

New initiatives may be possible in adult education. Any literacy campaign will need groups, leaders and (to a lesser extent) buildings: the churches could resume the significant role which they once played in spreading literacy. The health services in large parts of Namibia depend at present on the churches. After independence the government and people may look to the churches to resume medical work which has been usurped by the South African army. This could be an opportunity for the churches to move towards preventative primary health care, rather than just traditional curative medicine. Here there would be a clear link with adult education.

However, the most significant role of the churches may be as a source of lay leaders who are capable both of participation in reconstruction programmes and of recasting the work and institutions of the churches themselves.

Managing Social Tension

The government of a newly independent Namibia will have a unique opportunity for educational innovation. Yet these programmes will not meet all expectations, and conflicts will arise. We have already mentioned the possibility that parents may exert pressure for a purely quantitative expansion of schooling. If the former white schools remain better endowed with resources than others, the production of a small (albeit non-racial) stream of well-qualified school leavers will inevitably contrast with any goal of spreading the benefits of education. To the extent that transnational corporations continue to support elite schools, conflict may occur with them also.

Other clashes of interest can be predicted. There will be a tendency for different parts of the country and different social groups within the nation to use their political muscle to shift the allocation of educational resources in their direction. The 'new middle class' are likely to push for resources to go to more academically-orientated secondary schools for their children, rather than to rural primary schools or adult education.

Perhaps most seriously, teachers will be reluctant to lose the high salary differentials created by the South Africans. These have now been raised above a level which the country can afford for its public employees. The South African government, in its latest attempt to buy friends has therefore created a considerable problem for the incoming government, for if salaries are maintained at their present real level, teachers are in effect being unfairly rewarded compared with the rest of the community. Teachers may therefore have to be prepared for lower salaries. Increases may have to be earned not by long service, but by participation in in-service training courses, so that extra expenditure is balanced by improved quality of education. Opposition from some teachers can be expected.

In all these areas, the role of the state will be crucial in managing the tensions of disagreement. Two moves might ease the road to a resolution. Firstly things will be much clearer once the new government is in a position to define the detail of its education policies: the content of the new curriculum, and the timing of its introduction; criteria for deciding where new schools are to be built; allocation of resources to schooling, adult education, broadcasting, etc. Some guesswork is going to be necessary in making these decisions. Little accurate data is available. To improve its decision-making, there might be considerable advantage in the new ministry moving very early to establish a research and policy team which is responsible to the minister. Appointments to this body might be made without reference to the civil service commission, or whatever similar body there may be. If it is not possible to make such 'political' appointments, a research institute could perhaps be established outside government structures.

Secondly, an informed nationwide debate on education, engaging strong organisations of teachers, students, parents, and public employees, and possibly involving for example, a weekly radio programme, would promote a wide public understanding of educational issues. Such public awareness, which takes time and money to build up, would counter the risk of the education system being manipulated by privileged groups to their own advantage.

Priorities

It is time to return, in summary, to the main issues that will face the newly independent government of Namibia. Decisions on its priorities are obviously a matter for that government. There are alternatives, and much will depend on the circumstances and date of independence. However, from our analysis of the society and education systems that a new government will inherit, it may perhaps be worth drawing out one possible set of priorities for the reconstruction of Namibian education:

1. The establishment of a central team for research, coordination and planning of education, and generation of public debate and participation in educational transformation.
2. Teacher-training programmes, both part-time and full-time. In particular such programmes could improve linguistic abilities, especially in English, upgrade subject knowledge, and introduce methodologies for managing large classes.
3. A new curriculum, to be kept constantly under review, with an emphasis on the teaching of English and the development of production-related skills.
4. Identification and development of specific key skills, primarily through *in-service* training. In the longer run, specialist teaching and research institutes might be established for particular sectors of the economy.
5. Development of expertise and institutions in adult education, especially those concerned with literacy and the linking of literacy with political understanding, small development projects and women's groups.

Appendix

Proposals of the Advisory Committee for Human Sciences Research

In August 1983 the Advisory Committee submitted a five volume Report to the Department of National Education. A critique of the Report is printed on pp.45-49 above. This Appendix sets out in more detail, since the Report is only in Afrikaans, the proposals made for the establishment of a national education system in Namibia. Two important principles are firstly, that, education and vocational training must be combined and, secondly, that educational policy and support services must be centralised.

A new educational structure is proposed, including
- a one-year pre-primary course, to be taught in the afternoons by Sub A teachers;
- six years primary education (Sub A — Standard 4);
- transfer of the Standard 5 class (now in primary schools) to junior secondary schools, where a 3 year programme will be offered;
- three years of senior secondary education:
- tertiary education, including two-year diplomas and four-year degrees;
- adult and alternative educational provision for those who cannot directly utilise or link up with the main education system.

The objective of primary education, according to the Report, should be to ensure that all those who leave school are functionally literate, including the ability to understand, speak, read and write either English or Afrikaans, and to do simple calculations. Stress will also be placed on 'the modernisation of value-orientations', the development of skills to use simple equipment/tools, a healthy work-ethic, and knowledge of nutrition and personal hygiene. There should be a national certificate of functional literacy and basic skills which would offer access to routine semi-skilled jobs.

In addition, there should be an *entry* examination for junior secondary education dividing pupils into two streams. In *'ordinary'* junior secondary schools pupils would study 'appropriate subjects from traditional and vocational disciplines', leading to corresponding training at senior secondary level. An *alternative* junior secondary stream would train pupils in a particular vocational skill together with appropriate language and numeracy skills, so as to be able to work at 'operator level', or enter apprenticeship (after passing an entry examination).

Four kinds of senior secondary education are envisaged:
- Preparation for tertiary *Academic Education*, including logic, the natural sciences and mathematical methods, fluency in English or Afrikaans, internalisation of modern values and insight into the complexity of development.
- *Vocational or Career Education*, reconciling theoretical and practical education to provide skilled workers for technical trades, commerce, administration, and agriculture, with curricula and evaluation worked out in consultation with eventual employers.
- *Apprenticeship*: an alternative stream to the above, which would gradually be phased out on the grounds of expense.
- *Career Colleges*, which bridge secondary and tertiary phases to provide middle-level manpower, in technical fields, teaching, nursing, commerce, administration, and agriculture. At the end of such courses students could obtain a diploma, equivalent to two years of university education. The present Academy for Tertiary Education is looked upon as the model for such a college.

In tertiary (university) education it is proposed that the Academy for Tertiary Education should initially concentrate on diploma courses, and gradually develop relevant degree courses. The Academy should also initiate postgraduate research into the problems of development and of transitional cultures.

The report suggests that task forces should be set up to implement its proposals. The following programme of action is suggested:
- introduce career training colleges at senior secondary level, in collaboration with mining companies;
- reduce drop-outs from primary school by developing a new curriculum, including a pre-primary school-readiness year, and by a streaming (separate class) system which stops repetition of classes;
- use of school facilities for different purposes, especially career training, night schools and teacher training;
- centralise educational administration;

- replace 'leaving' with 'entry' examinations;
- develop an effective curriculum for functional literacy in English or Afrikaans:
- establish a central educational statistics service.

Statistical Supplement

Table 1

Number of Pupils in Different Classes 1981[1]

	Year	Standard	Black	Coloured	White	Total
				No. of Pupils		
PRIMARY	1	Sub A	55 101	5 261	1 712	62 074
	2	Sub B	35 078	4 507	1 693	41 278
	3	Std. 1	29 603	4 195	1 714	35 512
	4	Std. 2	21 259	3 609	1 837	26 705
	5	Std. 3	17 227	3 695	1 665	22 587
	6	Std. 4	12 390	3 154	1 669	17 213
	7	Std. 5	14 294	2 936	1 622	18 852
SECONDARY	8	Std. 6	5 176	2 684	1 486	9 346
	9	Std. 7	3 107	1 457	1 422	5 986
	10	Std. 8	3 047	952	1 206	5 205
	11	Std. 9	905	581	1 155	2 641
	12	Std.10	346	284	990	1 620
	Total		197 533	33 315	18 171	249 019

Note
1. This Table may not be accurate, especially as the central government grant to ethnic authorities depends in part on how many school-children they report.
Pupils in Walvis Bay are not included.

Source
Van Niekerk 1982, Advisory Committee for Human Sciences Research 1983.

Table 2

Numbers in School 1971-1981

Year	Blacks	Coloureds	Whites	Total
1971	99 846	20 174	22 473	142 493
1972	106 186	21 352	22 604	150 142
1973	116 320	22 097	22 781	161 198
1974	124 896	25 053	22 260	172 209
1975	134 551	27 118	22 488	185 157
1976	140 502	27 983	22 347	190 832
1977	152 384	27 517	22 281	202 182
1978	164 266	30 375	20 439	215 080
1979	175 549	29 743	19 397	224 689
1980	186 833	31 070	18 876	236 779
1981	197 533	33 315	18 171	249 019

Notes:
1. Including pupils enrolled for teacher-training and vocational training in schools.
2. These figures exclude Walvis Bay, (probably) from 1980 onwards.

Source
Advisory Committee for Human Sciences Research, 1983.

Table 3

Enrolments in Namibia and Botswana 1981

		Percentage of students in different school years	
	Year	Namibia	Botswana
Primary	1	25	15
	2	17	15
	3	14	13
	4	11	13
	5	9	10
	6	7	11
	7	8	13
Secondary	8	4	3
	9	2	3
	10	2	2
	11	1	0.8
	12	0.7	0.8

Source
Education Statistics 1981 (Botswana) and Table 1.

Table 4

Analysis of Black Enrolments 1980

Standard or Course	Male	Female	Total	% of Total
Sub A	26 519	26 899	53 418	28.59
Sub B	16 116	16 444	32 560	17.43
Std. 1	12 906	14 616	27 522	14.73
Std. 2	8 594	10 964	19 558	10.47
Subtotal lower primary	*64 135*	*68 923*	*133 058*	*71.22*
Std. 3	6 801	9 368	16 169	8.65
Std. 4	4 716	6 773	11 489	6.15
Std. 5	4 902	6 090	12 992	6.95
Subtotal higher primary	*16 419*	*24 231*	*40 650*	*21.75*
Std. 6	2 001	2 966	4 967	2.66
Std. 7	1 370	2 049	3 419	1.83
Std. 8	1 328	1 700	3 028	1.62
Subtotal junior secondary	*4 699*	*6 715*	*11 414*	*6.11*
Std. 9	338	206	544	0.29
Std. 10	206	137	343	0.18
Subtotal senior secondary	*544*	*343*	*887*	*0.47*
teacher training	242	331	573	0.31
technical training	97	—	97	0.05
social workers	9	7	16	0.008
Subtotal professional training	*348*	*338*	*686*	*0.308*
Disabled (special school)	84	54	138	0.07
Total	**86 229**	**100 604**	**186 833**	**100.00**

Source
Department of National Education statistics 1981.

Table 5

Teacher/Pupil Ratios

	Black Schools (1980)	Coloured Schools (1981)	White Schools (1981)
No of teachers	5 066[1]	1 207	1 362
No of pupils	186 833	33 315	18 171
No of pupils per teacher	37	28	13

Notes
1. 179 of these were white. 2 688 were female, and 2 378 male. In Ovamboland, a war zone, there were 1 772 black women teachers and only 777 men.

Sources
Van Niekerk, 1982, Annual Report of Education Branch of Administration for Whites, 1981; Dept of National Education.

Table 6

Estimates of Education Expenditure 1981/82[1]

(Rand)

	Total Expenditure	Expenditure per pupil
Black schooling	46 m.	232
Coloured schooling	10 m.	300
White schooling	22 m.	1 210
Academy for Tertiary Education	3 m.	
Government staff training	3½ m.	
Broadcasting	10 m.	
Total[2]	95 m.	

Notes
1. Includes capital expenditure.
2. Total education budget for 1982/83 about R128 m.

Sources
1981/82 Budget, Reports for White and Coloured Administrations, Human Sciences Report, and own estimates.

Table 7
Black Teachers' Salaries 1982 (Rand)[1]

Qualification		Annual starting salary	Salary per month[2]	Annual increment
Primary education, with	Male	1 590	132	(none)
no teacher training	Female	1 176	98	(none)
Std 8, no teacher training		2 760	230	300
Std 10, no teacher training		3 966	330	408
Std 6 and teacher training		3 150	262	408
Std 8 and teacher training		3 966	330	408
Std 10 and teacher training		5 190	432	540
Degree and teacher training		8 970	747	675
Primary School Principal		8 160	680	600
Head of Dept (Secondary School)		14 370	1 197	810

Notes
1. These figures were collected from private individuals, and it is believed that substantial further pay increases may have been awarded later in 1982.
2. For comparison, minimum wages were around R120 at Tsumeb mine and R230 at CDM mine.

Source
Miscellaneous.

Table 8
Black Teachers' Qualifications 1980
(Number)

Highest level of schooling passed	Teachers with teacher training	Teachers without teacher training	Total
Std. 6	1 957	1 998[1]	
Std. 8	758		
Std.10	127	29	
Degree	14	4	
Total	2 856	2 031	4 887

Note
1. About 22% or 440 of this number probably had std. 8, and the remainder std. 6 or less, judging by statistics for all teachers published by the Advisory Committee on Human Sciences Research 1983, Vol. 5, p.81.

Source
Department of National Education and Van Niekerk 1982.

Table 9
Academy for Tertiary Education Enrolments 1981

Course	Full-time Students		Part-time Students	
	Uncompleted Secondary Education	Completed Secondary Education	Uncompleted Secondary Education	Completed Secondary Education
Teacher Training	151	35	—	24
Social Work	7	12	—	—
Commerce (intensive)	—	7	—	—
Secretarial	—	23	—	63
Technical	53	8	47	16
Medical Technology	—	24	—	—
Std. 6 subjects	—	—	16	—
Std. 8 subjects	—	—	158	—
Std.10 subjects	—	—	233	—
Music	—	—	61	—
Practical Languages	—	—	73	—
Cultural Enrichment	—	—	80	—
Total	211	109	668	103

Source
Buitendacht, Report on Academy for Tertiary Education 1981.

Table 10
Namibian Students at South African Universities 1971-1978

	1971	1972	1973	1974	1975	1976	1977	1978
Whites	1 564	1 698	1 716	1 948	2 150	2 087	2 168	2 268
Coloureds								
At white universities	21	24	26	28	29	48	45	56
At coloured University of Western Cape	23	35	62	58	72	85	103	101
Total	44	59	88	86	101	133	148	157
Blacks								
At white universities	19	21	20	41	47	46	79	65
At black universities	28	34	31	35	37	49	33	33
Total	47	55	51	76	84	95	112	98

Source
Van Niekerk 1982

Table 11
Requirements[1] for Skilled Personnel at Independence

Sector	Present posts	Redundant[2]	New needs[3]	New total	Present Europeans[4]	New Expatriates	Total Namibians[5]	New posts
Agriculture[6]	10 000	1 000	1 500	10 500	750	1 250	8 500	4 500
Fishing	1 000	NR[7]	—	1 000	100	250	650	150
Mining	5 000	—	100	5 100	2 500	500	2 100	1 000
Manufacturing	3 000	750	250	2 500	1 000	500	1 000	500
Water and power	1 000	—	400	1 400	200	500	700	400
Construction	2 500	250	750	3 000	250	500	2 250	750
Transport	1 500	—	1 000	2 500	100	200	2 200	1 200
Communications	750	—	250	1 000	50	450	500	350
Commerce	5 000	2 250	250	3 000	650	250	2 100	600
Finance	500	—	250	750	150	200	400	300
Other services	1 750	250	250	1 750	500	—	1 250	250
Government[8]	18 000	8 000	12 500	22 500[10]	1 250	2 700	18 550	12 000
Administration[9]	*4 500*	*4 000*	*250*	*750*	*—*	*250*	*500*	*500*
Education	*6 500*	*1 500*	*6 250*	*11 250*	*500*	*1 250*	*9 500*	*6 000*
Health	*3 500*	*1 000*	*3 500*	*6 000*	*500*	*500*	*5 000*	*3 000*
Agriculture	*1 500*	*500*	*1 000*	*2 000*	*100*	*400*	*1 500*	*1 000*
Other[10]	*2 000*	*1 000*	*1 500*	*2 500*	*150*	*300*	*2 050*	*1 500*
TOTAL	50 000	12 500	17 500	55 000	7 500	7 300	40 200	22 000

1. These estimates include all managerial/administrative (10 000), professional/technical/para-professional (16 800), 75% supervisory/foreman (8 250), 75% skilled (4 750), 50% clerical/secretarial (3 250) and about 15% semi-skilled (7 000) personnel.
2. Posts either inappropriate, unnecessary or non-priority in an independent Namibia.
3. Posts relating to priority programme and institution requirements.
4. Includes personnel replaced by their employers (e.g. mining companies), by voluntary agencies (e.g. churches) and by new management contractors (e.g. for nationalised enterprises).
5. Present personnel total 20 000 of whom 2 000 assumed unavailable or unacceptable after independence, 22 000 promotions and new entries with, when possible, brief 'upgrading' and gap filling courses.
6. Excludes government agricultural services. See Note 8.
7. Special case. Immediate post-independence data assume the loss of the present fishing fleet and contracting foreign fleet with partially Namibian crews.
8. Includes government agricultural services, excludes police, prisons and armed forces.
9. Categories not comparable. Present posts figure includes 'Bantu Administration', 'Coloured Administration' and 'Security Forces' other than army (i.e. police, prisons).
10. Excludes army, police and prisons.

Source: United Nations Institute for Namibia, 1978.

Bibliography

Abrahams, Kenneth, 'The Döbra Students Conference', *The Namibian Review*, January-March 1983.
Abrahams, Kenneth, 'Whither Education in Namibia?', *The Namibian Review*, July-August 1983.
Abrahams, Yvette, 'The Emergence of a Namibian Student Movement', *The Namibian Review*, April-June 1983.
Academy for Tertiary Education, *General Information and Regulations 1983*, (Windhoek 1983).
Advieskomitee vir Geesteswetenskaplike Navorsing in SWA/Namibië (Advisory Committee for Human Sciences Research in SWA/Namibia, ACHSR), *Ondersoek na die onderwys in SWA/Namibië (Inquiry into Education in SWA/Namibia)* Verslag AGN1: Verslag van die komitee insake riglyne vir 'n stelsel van onderwysvoorsiening 1982. (Report *ACHSR 1*: Report of the committee on guidelines for an education system).
Verslag AGN 2: Verslag oor Demografie en onderwysstatistiek vir SWA/Namibië, C.J. Van Niekerk, 1982. (Report *ACHSR 2*: Report on demography and education statistics for SWA/Namibia).
Verslag AGN 3: Verslag van die navorsingsprojek-komitee: Kurrikulering, 1982. (Report *ACHSR 3*: Report of the reasearch project committee on curriculum development).
Verslag AGN 4: Verslag van die navorsingsprojek-komitee: Knelpunte in veeltalige onderwyssituasie, 1982. (Report *ACHSR 4*: Report on the research project committee: problem areas in multi-lingual education).
Verslag AGN 5: Verslag van die navorsingsprojek-komitee: Onderwysstelselbeplanning 1983. (Report *ACHSR 5*: Report of the research project committee: planning an education system).
Administration for Coloureds, *Annual Report: 1980/81*, (Representative Authority of the Coloureds).
Africa Bureau, *Black Education in South Africa*, Africa Bureau Document Paper No 32.
Ahmed, M. & Coombs, P.H., *Education for Rural Development: Case Studies for Planners*, (N.Y. Prager Publishers 1975).

Angula, A.N., *Elementary School Syllabus for Namibian Children*, SWAPO Department of Education and Culture (Lusaka, 1974).

Angula, A.N., *Programme Inviting Projects 1982*, SWAPO Department of Education and Culture (Luanda, 1982 a).

Angula, A.N., *The Relationship between Education and Society*, SWAPO Seminar on Education and Cuture for Liberation (Lusaka, 1982 b).

Angula, A.N., *Preliminary Perspectives into An Emergent Education System for Namibia*, Paper for 1982 SWAPO/Dag Hammarskjold Foundation Seminar on Education and Culture for Liberation in Namibia (Lusaka, Sept 20-25, 1982 c).

Angula, N., *English Usage in the Namibia Health and Education Centres: Some Reflections*, (paper from Commonwealth Secretariat/SWAPO Seminar (Lusaka, October 1983).

Archer, M.S., *Social Origins of Educational Systems*, (Sage Publications, London, 1979).

Beukes, A. & Boys, Aloys, *The 1982 Annual Report on Rural Community Development Work*, Council of Churches in Namibia, December 1982.

Blakemore, K. & Cooksey, B., *A Sociology of Education for Africa*, (George Allen and Unwin, London, 1981).

Brauer, H., *Report of Consultancy* (to Bureau of Literacy and Literature) photocopy, December 1980.

Brauer, H., *Evaluation Report, Bureau of Literacy and Literature*, photocopy (Windhoek June 1983).

Bryden, P.A., *Report on the First Pre-Teacher Training Course for Namibian Teachers at the Selly Oak Colleges*, (Birmingham, 1983).

Bryden, P.A., *Report on the Course for Namibian Students at the Selly Oak Colleges September 1980-July 1981*, Department of Social Studies, Selly Oak Colleges, (Birmingham 1981).

Buitendacht, A.J.H., *Annual Report 1981*, A Report on the Activities of the Academy for Tertiary Education for the period 1 January 1981 to 31 December 1981, Academy for Tertiary Education, 1981.

Carver, D., *Teacher Training and English Language Teaching in the Namibian Context*, paper from SWAPO/Commonwealth Secretariat Seminar (Lusaka, October 1983).

Castles, S. & Wüstenberit, W., *The Education of the Future: an Introduction to the Theory and Practice of Socialist Education*, (Pluto Press, London, 1979).

CIIR/BCC (Catholic Institute for International Relations/British Council of Churches), *Namibia in the 1980s*, (London, 1981).

CIIR (Catholic Institute for International Relations, *Mines and Independence*, A Future for Namibia 3: Mining (London, 1983).

Chamberlain, R., *English as the medium of official communication for Namibia: the implications for the future government*, Paper from SWAPO/Commonwealth Secretariat Seminar (Lusaka, October 1983).

Commonwealth Secretariat, *Distance Education Programme for Namibians*, Project Proposal (London, 1981).

Coombs, P. & Ahmed, M., *Attacking Rural Poverty: How Nonformal Education can help*, (Baltimore, The Johns Hopkins UP, 1979)

Coombs, P., *New paths to learning for rural children and youth*, International Council for Educational Development (New York, 1973).
Council of Churches in Namibia, *Statements by Namibian Churches*, (Windhoek, 1979)
Council of Churches in Namibia, *Continuing Education Projects*, mimeo, (Windhoek, 1980).
Cross, S., Dionisotti, G., et al., *A Select Development Bibliography of Namibia*, Food and Agriculture Organisation, 1981.
Crowley, D., Etherington, A., Kidd, R., *Mass Media Manual, How to Run a Radio Learning Group Campaign*, (Friedrich-Ebert-Stiftung, Bonn 1978)
Department of Education and Culture (N. Angula), *Education for the Future: Programmes, Prospects and Needs. The Education Programme of SWAPO of Namibia*, Paper from Commonwealth Secretariat/SWAPO Seminar (Lusaka, 19-27 October 1983).
Department of National Education, *Monthly Circular April 1982*.
Department of National Education, *Onderwys vir Swartes in Suidwes-Afrika Statistiek Maart 1979, (Education for blacks in South West Africa Statistics March 1979)*.
Department of National Education, *Onderwys vir swartes in Suidwes-Afrika Statistiek vir 1980, (Education for blacks in South West Africa Statistics 1980)*.
Department of Social Studies, Selly Oak Colleges, *Report on the Course for Namibian Students at the Selly Oak Colleges September 1981-July 1982*.
Dore, R., *The Diploma Disease, Education Qualification and Development*, (George Allen and Unwin, London, 1978).
Doyle, M.V., 'Adult Literacy Education in Namibia', in *Community Development Journal*, Vol. 14, No. 2 (1979).
Drechsler, H., *Let Us Die Fighting, The Struggle of the Herero and Nama against German Imperialism (1884-1915)*, (Zed Press, London, 1980).
Dumont, R., & Cohen, N., *The Growth of Hunger, A New Politics of Agriculture*, (Marion Boyars, London, 1980).
Education Branch (white) SWA Administration, *Annual Report 1981*.
Ellis, J., *Formal and Nonformal Education in Namibia*, Dissertation submitted in part fulfilment for the Diploma in Adult Education at Manchester University, May 1980.
Ellis, J., *Basic Adult Education in Namibia after Independence*, MEd thesis, Manchester University, 1981,
Fauvet, P., 'Education in Angola', *People's Power No. 15*, Mozambique, Angola, and Guinea Information Centre, (London, Winter 1979).
Freire, Paulo., 'To the Coordinator of a 'cultural circle' (in Chile)' *Convergence*, Vol. 14, No. 1, 1971.
Freire, Paulo., *Education: the Practice of Freedom*, (1967 & 1969), (Writers and Readers, London, 1976).
Freire, Paulo., *Cultural Action for Freedom*, (1970), (Penguin 1977).
Freire, Paulo., *Pedagogy of the Oppressed*, (1972), (Penguin 1978).
Freire, Paulo., *Pedagogy in Process. The Letters to Guinea Bissau*, (Seabury NY, 1978).
Ganhao, F., 'The Struggle Continues: Mozambique's Revolutionary

Experience in Education', *Development Dialogue*, 1978: 2.
German Development Institute, *Multi-Sectoral Study on Namibia — Summary*, (West Berlin, 1978).
German Development Institute, *Perspectives of Independent Development in Southern Africa, The Cases of Zimbabwe and Namibia*, (West Berlin, 1980)
Gibellini, R. (ed.), *Frontiers of Theology in Latin America*, (SCM Press, London, 1980).
Goody, J., *Literacy in Traditional Societies*, (1968) (Cambridge University Press, 1975).
Gordon, Robert J., *Mines, Masters and Migrants*, (Ravan Press, Johannesburg, 1977).
Goulet, Denis., *Looking at Guinea-Bissau: a new nation's development strategy*, Overseas Development Council, 1978.
Green, R.H., 'The Unforgiving Land — Basis for a Post-Liberation Programme in Namibia', *Bulletin*, IDS, Sussex, September 1980, Vol. 11 No. 4.
Green, R.H., Kiljunen K. & M.L., *Namibia The Last Colony*, (Longman, London, 1981).
Guile, Timothy, *English in Non-formal Education: A Report on the Adult Education Program at CDM Oranjemund, Namibia 1976-79*, photocopy of lecture, 1980.
Haikali, E., *Annual report for the Namibian Social and Chaplaincy Service 1980*, chaplaincy to Namibians (Lusaka, December 1980).
Hastings, A., *A History of African Christianity 1950-1975*, (Cambridge University Press, 1979).
Howell, Gareth, *The Education of Namibians*, mimeo, Overseas Development Ministry, 1978.
Hoyles, M., *The Politics of Literacy*, (Writers and Readers, London, 1977).
Hunke, Heinz, *Namibia — the strength of the powerless*, (IDOC International, Rome, 1980).
International Seminar on Educational Alternatives for Southern Africa, Summary Conclusions, *Development Dialogue*, 1978: 2.
Kahler, David (ed.), *International Seminar on Curriculum Development for Basic Education Programmes*, German Foundation for International Development and International Institute for Adult Literacy Methods 1978, DOK 969 A/a.
Kelly, G.A., *The Psychology of Personal Constructs*, Vol. 1, (Norton, 1955)
Kiljunen, Kimmo, 'Namibia: the Ideology of National Liberation', *Bulletin*, IDS Sussex September 1980, Vol. 11, No. 4.
Kindervatter, Suzanne, *Nonformal Education as an Empowering Process*, Centre for International Education (Massachusetts, 1979).
King, Kenneth, *The African Artisan, Education and the Informal Sector in Kenya*, (Heinemann 1977).
Kinsey, B.H., *Namibia: a data profile on agriculture, food, nutrition and rural development*, Food and Agriculture Organisation 1981.
Kinsey, B.H. & Muir, K.A., *Agriculture, Food and Rural Development in Namibia: a Select Annotated Bibliography*, FAO, 1981.

Kuhanga, N., 'Education and Self-Reliance in Tanzania: a National Perspective', *Development Dialogue*, 1978: 2.
Lachenmann, G., *Namibia Sektorstudie Bildungswesen*, German Development Institute, West Berlin, 1979.
Liberation Support Movement (ed.), *Namibia: SWAPO Fights for Freedom*, LSM Information Centre (California, 1978).
Long, Norman, *An Introduction to the Sociology of Rural Development*, (Tavistock Publications, London, 1977).
Mackie, R. (ed.), *Literacy and Revolution: the Pedagogy of Paulo Freire*, (Pluto Press, London, 1980).
Majiedt, S.J., *Onderwys en Opleiding as 'n Noodsaaklike inset tot Sosio-Ekonomiese Ontwikkeling* Referaat, Sosio—Ekonomiese Beraad, Windhoek 11 Augustus, 1982.
Mbamba, A. Mauno, *The Namibia Education and Health Centres — a study of SWAPO schools among Namibian refugees in Zambia and Angola*, Institute of International Education, University of Stockholm, November 1979.
Mbamba, A. Mauno, 'Primary Education for an Independent Namibia: planning in a situation of uncertainty and instability', *Studies in Comparative and International Education No. 5*, (Almquist and Wiksell, Stockholm, 1982.)
Mbamba, A. Mauno, *Primary Education for an Independent Namibia*, paper presented at a seminar on Education and Culture for Liberation (Lusaka, 1982).
McEldowney, Patricia L., *Report on English in Namibia*, mimeo, Selly Oak Colleges, 1978.
Melber, Henning, *Schule und Kolonialismus: das formale Erziehungswesen Namibias*, Institut für Afrika-Kunde (Hamburg, 1979).
Melber, Henning, *General Notes on Exercises/Test Material*, Project: Political geography of Namibia, 1982.
Mercer, Dennis (ed.), *Breaking Contract — the story of Vinnia Ndadi*, LSM Information Center (Canada, 1974).
Moodie, T. Dunbar, *The Rise of Afrikanerdom: Power, Apartheid and the Afrikaner civil religion*, (University of California Press, 1980).
Moorsom, Richard, *Transforming a Wasted Land*, A Future for Namibia, 2: Agriculture (CIIR, London, 1982).
Mozambique, Angola and Guinea Information Centre, *MPLA First Congress and Theses on Education*, (MAGIC, London, 1979).
Mthoko, N., *Distance Education Programme for Namibians*, Namibian Extension Unit (Lusaka, 1982).
National Adult Education Programme, *Training of Adult Education Functionaries — a handbook*, Directorate of Adult Education, Ministry of Education and Social Welfare, Government of India (New Delhi, 1978).
National Education Act 1980, (AG 196 of 1980), *Official Gazette Extraordinary*, 31 December 1980.
Ngavirue, Z., 'Careers in SWA Namibia', *Education and Training Series — No. 1*, Private Sector Foundation (Windhoek, 1982).
Niehoff, R.O. (ed.), *Nonformal Education and the Rural Poor*, (Michigan

State University, 1977).
Nouiseb, M., *A Descriptive Account of the Operations of the Churches' English Language Project*, paper, 1983.
Nyerere, Julius, 'Education and Liberation', *Development Dialogue* 1974: 2.
Nyerere, Julius, *The Arusha Declaration: ten years after*, (Government Printer, Dar es Salaam, 1977).
Oakley, Peter, 'Participation in Development in N.E. Brazil', *Community Development Journal*, Vol. 15, No. 2 (1980).
O'Callaghan, Marion, *Namibia: the effects of apartheid on culture and education*, UNESCO (Paris, 1977).
Ombuze, Ya Namibia., (SWAPO), *Student Unrest in Namibia*, mimeo, 1976.
Oxenham, J., *Nonformal Education Approaches to Teaching Literacy*, (Michigan State University, 1975).
Price, R.F., *Education in Modern China*, (Routledge and Kegan Paul, London, 1979).
Regulations made under the National Education Act, 1980, regarding School Committees at Government Schools, (AG73 of 1982), *Official Gazette Extraordinary*, 15 May 1982.
Riddell, Roger, *Education for Employment*, No. 9 of From Rhodesia to Zimbabwe (CIIR, London, 1980).
Robson, Mike, 'Production in Schools', *Teachers' Forum*, (Zimbabwe, April 1982).
Segal, R. & First, R., *South West Africa: Travesty of Trust*, (Deutsch, London, 1967).
Seminar on Education in Zimbabwe: Past, Present and Future, Salisbury August 27-September 7, 1981, News and Notes in *Development Dialogue*, Uppsala, 1982: 1-2.
Scott, Michael, *A Time to Speak*, (Faber and Faber, 1958).
Shejavali, Abisai, *The Ovambo-Kavango Church*, (Helsinki, 1970).
Simpson, C., 'Life in a Frelimo School', *People's Power*, No. 12, Autumn-Winter 1978).
South African Labour Bulletin, *Focus on Namibia*, Double Issue, January-February 1978, Vol. 4, Nos. 1 & 2.
SWA/Namibia Survey, Press Relations Office of Administrator General (Windhoek, June 1980).
South West Africa People's Organisation, *SWAPO Seminar on Literacy: To study strategies, techniques, methods and content towards establishment of a national literacy programme for an independent Namibia*, Lusaka, Zambia, May 1978, (SWAPO, 1979).
SWAPO Women's Council, *Literacy Among Namibian Women*, Document, January 1980.
SWAPO, Department of Information and Publicity, *To be Born a Nation: The Liberation Stuggle in Namibia*, (Zed Press, London 1982).
Thomas, Wolfgang, H., *Economic Development in Namibia*, (Kaiser-Grünewald, 1978).
Tjitendero, M.P., *Policy Options for Basic Education*, paper presented at SWAPO Seminar on Education, Lusaka, 1982.
Tjitendero, M.P., Untitled, draft paper on education policy for an

independent Namibia, (Lusaka, 1982).
Tjongarero, D.J.K., *The Role of the Black Student in Changing the Southern Africa situation*, mimeo, 1977.
Tlhabanello, Mokganedi, M., *The Alternative to the South African 'Bantu Universities'*, (mimeo) 1976.
Tötemeyer, Gerhard, *Namibia Old and New, Traditional and Modern Leaders in Ovamboland*, (C. Hurst, London, 1978).
Troup, F., *In Face of Fear, Michael Scott's Challenge to South Africa*, (Faber and Faber, 1950).
United Nations Institute for Namibia, *Prospectus 1979, Prospectus 1980*, (Lusaka, 1979, 1980).
United Nations Institute for Namibia, *Report of the Senate of UNIN to the United Nations Council for Namibia and the Secretary General of the UN*, (1977, 1978, 1979).
United Nations Institute for Namibia, (Green, R.H.) *Manpower Estimates and Development Implications for Namibia* (Lusaka, 1978).
United Nations Institute for Namibia, (Mshonga, S.), *Toward Agrarian Reform, Policy Options for Namibia*, (Lusaka, 1979).
United Nations Institute for Namibia, (Chamberlain, R.; Diallo, A. & John. E.), *Toward a Language Policy for Namibia: English as the Official Language: Perspectives and Strategies*, (Lusaka, Zambia, 1981).
United Nations Institute for Namibia, (Tjitendero, M.), *Education Policy Planning for Independent Namibia*, Working paper for seminar, Lusaka, April, 28-30, 1981.
Van Niekerk, C.J., 1982, See Advieskomitee vir Geesteswetenskaplike Navorsing in SWA/Namibië.
Van Rensburg, P., *Report from Swaneng Hill: Education and Employment in an African Country*, Dag Hammarskjöld Foundation (Uppsala, 1974).
Vella, J.K., *Learning to Listen*, Centre for International Education, (Massachusetts, 1979).
Vesper, Michael, *Zur Funktion der Homelands in Namibia*, paper, Department of Sociology, University of Bielefeld, 1979.
Winter, Colin O'Brien, *Namibia — the story of a Bishop in Exile*, (Eerdmands, Grand Rapids, USA, 1977).
World University Service, (UK), *Seminar on Education for Namibians in the UK, June 7, 1982, Report*.
Ya-Otto, John, with Gjerstad, O. & Mercer, M., *Battlefront Namibia*, (Heinemann, 1982).
Zimbabwe Foundation for Education with Production, *New Schools to Transform Zimbabwe*, (ZIMFEP, 1982).
Zimbabwe African National Union, Education and Culture Department, *Lecture on Philosophy of Education*, (Mozambique, 1978).
Zimbabwe African National Union, Education and Culture Department, *Education Planning*, (Mozambique, 1979).